The Sons
of the Wind

*The Sacred Stories
of the Lakota*

The Sons
of the Wind

*The Sacred Stories
of the Lakota*

*Introduction by
Vivian Arviso One Feather*

*Edited by D.M. Dooling
from the
James R. Walker Collection*

Parabola Books

Third printing, 1988.

Copyright © 1984 by
The Society for the Study of Myth and Tradition
656 Broadway, New York, N.Y. 10012

With the cooperation of
the Colorado Historical Society
200 Fourteenth Avenue, Denver, Colorado

PARABOLA BOOKS are published by the Society for the Study of
Myth and Tradition, a non-profit organization devoted to the dis-
semination and exploration of materials relating to the myth, sym-
bol, ritual, and art of the great religious traditions. The Society also
publishes PARABOLA, The Magazine of Myth and Tradition.

Library of Congress Number: 84-061403
ISBN: 0-930407-00-8

Contents

Introduction

D.M. Dooling presents in the following pages the sacred beginnings of the Lakota Nation, a treasured knowledge that has been held for generations only by Holy Men who have been entrusted with such responsibility. It is in these sacred origins that the Lakota Nation find their life-essence, the source of power and direction throughout history which has enabled their spiritual leaders to marshal the people.

It is very difficult to isolate a term which best describes the collective powers in the Lakota universe. These powers are godlike and have spiritual qualities which are individually unique. The term "Sacred Beings" is perhaps the best English expression for this collective entity and is used throughout this text as well as "Spirits," a much less adequate word.

In a very simplified and yet profound manner, the basic guiding principles of Lakota culture are portrayed through the lives of these Sacred Beings. Unashamed of their surly and pouting behavior, these Sacred Beings continually tested the limits of their own powers. They coped with inner family quarrels, had strained relations in their marriages, and had to contend with those among themselves who desired greater powers. Ironically, even as they resolved their conflicts, they discovered newer conflicts within the solution. Time after time, Skan resolved these situations, meting out swift and harsh judgments that became binding for all time. In compliance, the Sacred Beings made amends and worked harder for the benefit of Lakota mankind.

In this formative period of the Lakota Nation, animals are people and people are animals. The Pte Oyate (Buffalo People) are the ancestors of the shaggy buffalo that provided sustenance to mankind after having served the Sacred Beings in the regions under the earth. It is from this same underworld region that Tokahe (First Man) was lured to the earth's surface through a risk-taking transition that held the promise of a better life. Once here, Tokahe and his followers were abandoned and forced to fend for themselves. They survived only with the aid of the Sacred Beings;

eventually they prospered and built a nation of highly respected people known as Wicasa Ikce, the common men.

Today, the Lakota Nation continues to thrive in a world bounded by the four cardinal directions as set by the sons of Tate. Their concept of time as described in the establishment of the First, Second, Third, and Fourth Times is a practical part of their lives. In fact, the usage of the term Third Time, a moon, has reached far beyond the Lakota to become a vernacular expression describing a month. These modern descendants of Tokahe continue to offer their prayers and seek visions as instructed by the Holy Men of long ago.

The presence of the Sacred Beings is a part of the everyday existence of the Lakota Nation. The lightning and thunderous voice of Wakinyan is seen, felt, and heard through the power of the cleansing rains that sweep over the earth. In protecting their young against the evil effect of Anog-Ite (Double Face Woman), Lakota mothers still make turtle amulets. Elsewhere, the infinitesimal *mini-watu* (microbes) await the opportunity to torment their next victim.

As messengers of the Sacred Beings, the sons of Tate, Eya, Yata, Yanpa, Okaga, and little Yum, continue to receive the prayers of the Lakota Nation. They maintain their ever constant vigil to provide guidance and consolation to all modern descendants of the Pte people.

I would like to commend D.M. Dooling for her efforts in sharing the knowledge that Sword and other Lakota Holy Men determined should be preserved for future generations through their transcriptions made and given to James Walker nearly a hundred years ago. It is an honorable gesture that the Lakota Nation be the first to be represented in this series of books to be published by PARABOLA.

My personal perspective is to stress the urgency of sharing this knowledge. My children, being of Lakota descent, were raised within the social traditions of their father's *tiospaye* (community). This particular *tiospaye* is proud of its history of having produced strong leaders among the Oglala Lakota on the Pine Ridge Indian Reservation in South Dakota. Like other concerned parents, I desire that my children understand and develop a deeper appreciation of their human existence and mature with the knowledge that the Lakota Nation began, not with the arrival of Columbus, but with the creation of this universe. And more importantly, they comprehend that as a people the Lakota Nation will endure indefinitely.

As a teacher of Lakota high school and college students, I have placed particular emphasis upon the creation of the Lakota universe. When every Lakota person preserves this knowledge, it ensures the continuation of the Lakota Nation. This spiritual knowledge provides a bastion of support enabling its students to weather the hardships of this world. For all these reasons, I encourage you, the reader, to be a full participant in the timeless teachings exposed in the succeeding pages. Approached with an open mind, they will enrich and fortify your interest in the physical as well as the cosmic worlds we live in.

Vivian Arviso One Feather
April 1984
Navajo Community College

Foreword

The Sons of the Wind is the mythology of the Oglala Lakota, that historic and still living tribe of the Sioux Nation who are the people of Crazy Horse, Red Cloud, and Black Elk, of the Little Big Horn and Wounded Knee. It is the epic account of how it all began: the first stirring of loneliness in the heart of matter, the longing for relationship in the very rock, Inyan himself; the appearance of the Spirits and the animals and the first holy people, the friends and servants of the High Powers; the making of the four times and the four directions, and all the increasing elaboration of relationships and their checks and balances until the coming on earth of the Real People, the Ikce Oyate—and the consequent loss, left behind "under the earth," of another knowledge and another nature.

This is not a book for scholars; they already have a splendid presentation of the exact, though still somewhat fragmented, basic texts of Dr. Walker's transcriptions with an excellent commentary, in Elaine Jahner's *Lakota Myth* (Univ. of Nebraska Press, 1983), and I leave to them the questions of provenance and authenticity which are their province. This is a book for lovers of myth; and whoever it was who first conceived these symbolic tales, for me there is no doubt that "their Authors are in Eternity." How much was invented by Dr. Walker in his effort to put together into a consecutive whole the scattered fragments he received from his Sioux informants? No one can ever really know, nor whether they were partly the original creations of some of the old men, the poetic Sword, for example. No one will ever be able to tell us whether these are in fact the stories that were told in the long evenings of the winter camps throughout Lakota history, or whether (as Walker himself believed) they may have come from a time so far in the past, so long before the coming of white people, that they had been forgotten by all but the shamans, who knew and transmitted them only to the dwindling number of their initiates.

We do know that when Dr. Walker came to the reservation at Pine Ridge, five years before the turn of the century and six years after Wounded Knee, there was only a handful left of the old shamans, with no pupils at all. Coming as a doctor faced with an impossible task, Walker called for the help of the medicine men to work with him against the epidemic of tuberculosis and other illnesses that were decimating the Lakota tribe. Gradually the old men took him into their confidence, taught him their secret language, and passed on to him the lore of their people. After Walker had left the reservation and not very long before his own death, he wrote: "Not one Oglala shaman remains alive, unless I except myself. It is probable that no Oglala today knows the mythology of his ancestors as held by the shamans."*

Earlier he had written, in a letter to the anthropologist Clark Wissler: "While no Indian has been able to give me the complete mythology in a systematic way, I have gotten quite a complete system of it piece-meal which I am attempting to systematize in a manner approved by the older Indians who are probably as good authority on it as exists."**   He died before finishing the task, and left behind him a mass of unpublished typescripts and variant versions of the same myths.

A beautiful rendering of the myths based on this material was published in a mimeographed edition in 1972 by the Oglala Sioux Culture Center of the Red Cloud Indian School at Pine Ridge, under the supervision of Vivian Arviso One Feather. A copy of this book was given me a few years later by Arthur Amiotte, the Oglala artist, whose Holy Elk shield is on our cover. He was then teaching at Little Eagle School on the Standing Rock reservation and using Vivian Arviso's book in his classroom; for

---

* "The Plains Indians, Their Medicines and Myths" — Colorado Historical Society, File Folder 69. Quoted by Jahner, op. cit., page 4.
** May 28, 1911. Quoted by Jahner, op. cit., page 7.

whether or not the myths as recounted by Dr. Walker were in the past a living part of the Lakota oral tradition, they are becoming so now; these are the tales the Lakotas are telling their children today.

Since it was to Vivian Arviso's work and Arthur Amiotte's introduction to it that I owe my first acquaintance with these marvelous stories, I feel a special gratitude to them both for that as well as for their continuing goodwill and help in preparing the present book. My contribution seems to me to have been only in trying to carry to completion Dr. Walker's intention, letting the stories find their way into a connected whole, and editing and smoothing over certain inconsistencies of detail and style. Nevertheless, I am sure that willy-nilly something that is personal to my own appreciation and understanding has crept in to shape my retelling, and so added another shading of interpretation to those of each of the others who have told these tales before me. It is an inevitable part of the process of myth's transmission that all its lovers leave in it something of their own substance.

My thanks are also due to Margot Honart West of the Colorado Historical Society in Denver, who has been most friendly and helpful in making the appropriate folders of the Walker material available to me, and also to Stephen Catlett of the American Philosophical Society in Philadelphia, for help with other manuscripts left by Dr. Walker.

I wish again to refer to Elaine Jahner's important book *Lakota Myth*, which has been of the greatest help to me, and to which all readers of this book who wish to know more of its origins must necessarily turn. I thank her also personally for her generous help in reading and commenting on the present text and for her advice on Lakota orthography as well as many details of the stories themselves. I wish that I could equally personally thank that remarkable man, James Walker, and his friends, the great old men of the Oglala Sioux: Finger, Sword, Little Wound, Short Bull, American Horse, Gray Goose, Left Heron, Lone Star, Bad

Wound . . . . They have all gone beyond my wish to express my gratitude and to be forgiven, whatever my errors or presumption in trying to bring these great true stories to my own people. Surely they all know now, more clearly than ever, the reality of the Lakota password, *"Mitakuye oyasin"* — "We are all related."

Glossary

A brief approximation to Lakota pronunciation is as follows:

a is broad as in *father*

e is pronounced *ay* as in *pay*

i is pronounced *ee*

u is like *oo* in *cook*

c is pronounced *ch*

g between vowels: *kh* (like German *machen*)

j: *jh* (as in *fusion*)

n following a vowel is not pronounced as the *n* sound in English, but nasalizes the vowel, as in French: e.g., *an* is pronounced as in French *blanc*. In this table, this sound is represented by ŋ.

k is sometimes like *g* in *good*

p is sometimes like *b*

s is sometimes *sh*

t is sometimes like *d*, or as *t* in *stop*

(See Buechel's Lakota Dictionary.)

Akan: see *kan*

Anog Ite: (an-óg ee-dáy) Double-faced.

Anpetu: (aŋ-báy-doo) Light, daylight. "The red that shines."

Ate: (ah-dáy) Father.

Eya: (áy-ah) To say anything. The West Wind.

Gnaski: (g-násh-gee) The demon. Son of Unk and Iya.

Hanhepi: (haŋ-háy-bee) Darkness, night.

Hanwi: (haŋ-wée) The moon.

Heyoka: (hay-yó-ka) Trickster, contrary. The other self of Wakinyan, who under this aspect is the spirit of growth and birth, and is called by Walker "the Restorer." See "The Wisdom of the Contrary"—an interview with Joseph Epes Brown, PARABOLA, Vol. IV, No. 1.

hunka: (húŋ-kah) Relative.

Hunku: (hoóŋ-koo) Mother.

Hu Nunpa: (hoó noóŋ-pah) Two legs. The bear.

Ibom: (ee-bóm) The cyclone. A name for Iya at his most violent.

Ikce: (eek-cháy) Common, natural, real. Ikce Oyate: (eek-cháy o-yáh-day) The real ones, the real people.

Iktomi: (eek-dó-mee) Spider; the Trickster.

Inyan: (eéŋ-yaŋ) Stone.

Ite: (ee-dáy) Face.

Iya: (eé-yah) Monster.

inipiti: (een-éeb-ee-tee) Sweat lodge.

kan: (kaŋ) Strange, wonderful, ancient, sacred. *-akan*, (ah-káŋ), word particle added to denote these qualities.

Keya: (káy-ah) Turtle.

Ksa: (k-sáh) Wisdom.

Ksapela: (k-sáh-pay-lah) Little wisdom.

Maka: (mah-káh) Earth. Maka-akan: (mah-káh ah-káng) earth spirit.

Mini Watu: (m-née wad-dóo) Stagnant water.

nagi: (nah-khée) Spirit. The *nagi, nagila, niya,* and *sicun* are the four aspects of the spirit or soul. Walker calls the *nagi* "the spirit that advises the conduct of each being." Amiotte calls it the ghost or double*, and according to George Sword, "The *nagi* of an animate being is its spirit and of an inanimate thing that grows from the ground is its smoke. This is the potency of anything."** It is given by Skan.

nagila: (nah-khée-lah) Spirit. The particle of the energy of Taku Skanskan which is in each being.*

niya: (nee-yáh) To breathe. "The life breath of a being" (Amiotte*). "Ghost that is the breath of life and witness to the advice the spirit gives" (Walker). Given by Tate.

Okaga: (o-káh-khah) The South Wind.

Oyate: (o-yáh-day) A people, nation.

Pahin: (pah-heeng) Porcupine.

Pte Oyate: (p-táy o-yáh-day) Buffalo people.

sicun: (see-chóong) Spirit; "that in man which is spirit and guards him against evil spirits." (Buechel). The power to produce offspring, health, and growth (Walker). The individual energy-power peculiar to each being (Amiotte*). Given by Wakinyan/Heyoka.

---

* Arthur Amiotte, "Our Other Selves." PARABOLA, Vol. VII, No. 2
** *Lakota Belief and Ritual*, ed. R.J. DeMallie and E. A. Jahner, U. of Nebraska Press, 1980.

Skan: (shkaŋg) "To do, to act, to move about" (Buechel). The active, moving principle; energy. According to Walker, Skan is the shamanic term for Taku Skanskan, and is the sky but also an omnipresent Spirit that gives life and motion to every living thing.*

Sunk: (shoonk) Dog.

Taku Skanskan: (dáh-goo shkaŋg-shkaŋg) The Great Spirit; "that which causes everything to move" (Buechel).

tanka: (táŋg-gah) Great.

Tatanka: (tah-táŋg-gah) Buffalo bull.

Tate: (tah-dáy) The wind.

Tatuyetopa: (tah-dóo-yay-dó-bah) The four quarters.

Tokahe: (toh-gáh-hay) The first.

Tokapa: (toh-gáh-pah) First-born.

Unhcegi: (oong-cháy-khee) Prehistoric animal; monster.

Unk: (oong) Walker says she is Passion, or Dissension. (Could it be from *unca*, to mock; "the Mocker"?)

Unktehi: (oong-tay-hee) Water monsters; the offspring of Unk and Unhcegi.

Wakanka: (wah-káŋg-gah) The Old Woman.

wakan: (wah-káŋg) Mysterious, incomprehensible, sacred.

Wakan Tanka: (wah-káŋg táŋg-kah) The Great Mysterious, the Great Incomprehensible.

Wakinyan: (wah-kéeng-yang) Thunder. The dual Spirit; under this aspect he is terrifying and destructive, but his other self,

---

*Letter from Walker to Wissler, Jan. 13, 1915, quoted by Jahner, op. cit., page 9.

Heyoka, has the beneficent side of the laughter-loving clown. (See *Heyoka*.)

waniyetu: (wah-née-yay-doo) Year.

Wata: (wáh-dah) Boat.

Wazi: (wah-zée) Pine tree. The Old Man of the North, the Wizard.

Wi: (wee) The Sun. Wi-a-kan, (wee-ah-káng) The sun spirit.

Woope: (wó-pay) Order, harmony, law; the Mediator.

Yanpa: (yáng-pah) The east wind.

Yata: (yáh-tah) The north wind.

Yumnimni (Yum): (yoom-néem-ni) To whirl. The little whirlwind or dust devil.

The First
Two Times

*This was the beginning
before there was time.
This was the beginning of
the world and of the sky
over the world...*

In the beginning was Inyan, who had no beginning, for he was there when there was no other, only Hanhepi, the Darkness. Inyan was soft and shapeless, but he was everywhere and he had all the powers. These powers were in his blood, and his blood was blue. His spirit was Wakan Tanka.

Inyan desired that there be others so that he might exercise his powers. But there could be no others unless he created them from himself. To do so he would have to give part of his spirit and part of his blood, and the powers that were in the blood. So he decided to create another but only as part of himself, so that he could keep control over the powers. He took part of himself and spread it over and around himself in the shape of a great disk. He named the disk Maka, the Earth, and he gave Maka a spirit, Maka-akan, Earth Spirit, and she is part of Inyan. But in creating her, he took so much from himself that his veins opened and all his blood flowed from him, and he shrank and became hard and powerless.

As Inyan's blood flowed, it became the blue waters which are on the earth. Because powers cannot live in water, they separated themselves and became a great blue dome whose edge is near the edge of Maka. This blue dome of the powers of the blood of Inyan is now the sky and is not material but is the spirit of Taku Skan-skan, the Great Spirit. When these powers assumed one shape, they said a voice spoke, saying: "I am the source of energy, I am Skan." This was the beginning of the third of the Sacred Beings who is the highest of all because he is spirit. Inyan and Maka are material, and the world of matter has no powers except what are given by Skan.

In time, Maka became quarrelsome and scolded Inyan because he had not created her as a separate being but only as a part of himself. She complained also that she could not control the waters that were upon her, and that because Hanhepi, the Darkness, was everywhere, she could not see herself, nor Inyan, nor Skan. She demanded that Inyan send Hanhepi away, but he replied that since all his blood had flowed from him in creating her, he was powerless. Then she taunted and nagged him until he said, "We shall take your complaint to Skan, who has all the powers I once had, and do as he says."

Skan heard the complaint of Maka and uttered the first decree: "Maka must remain as she was created, joined to Inyan as a part of the world, but she shall be able to see herself and control the waters."

Thus Skan was established as the final judge of all things.

Skan divided Hanhepi into two halves. One remained darkness and was banished to the regions under the world. From the other, Skan created Anpetu, the Light. He placed Anpetu on the world in place of Hanhepi and commanded him to make all things visible. Then there was light everywhere in the world, but there was no shadow or heat.

Maka saw herself and cried, "How bare I am, and how cold and ugly!" Then she saw the blue waters, and she divided them into seas and lakes and rivers, and wore them to adorn herself.

But after a time she complained again to Skan.

She said, "I cannot bear this brightness, and I am cold. I beg you, create something to warm me and to soften the light."

Then Skan took from Inyan, from Maka, from the waters, and from himself something from which he created a great shining disk. He named the disk Wi, the Sun, and gave him a spirit, Wi-akan, the Sun Power. This was the beginning of the fourth Sacred Being, but he was created by Skan, so he is a creature. Skan placed Wi above the blue dome of himself and commanded him to shine and give heat.

All the world was made hot, and again Maka was discontented and ordered Wi to make shadows, but Wi replied that he would obey only Skan. Skan heard the dispute and commanded Wi to give shadows to every material thing, but not to any spirit thing, and Wi did as Skan commanded. Skan declared, "The shadow of each thing shall be its spirit and shall be with it always."

Maka still complained. "The heat scorches me and the shadows irritate me," she said. "Return Hanhepi to the world so that I may have relief from the light and the shadows." And Wi also complained, "I have no rest and I am very tired. I also beg you to return Hanhepi to the world for some of the time so that I may rest while she is there."

Then Skan decreed: "Time shall be divided into two equal parts, daytime and nighttime. Anpetu shall have the daytime which shall be the time of activity, and Hanhepi shall follow him with the nighttime which shall be the time of rest. Each daytime Wi shall come up over the edge of the world and make a journey across the sky and each nighttime he shall go down over the edge of the world into the regions under the world to rest there."

So the first two times were established, and Maka was warmed and cooled and made more comfortable. But after a time she complained again because she was not bright red like Wi nor blue like Skan, but had no color. And again Skan listened to her, and gave her the color green and to Inyan the color yellow.

Then Skan assembled the Sacred Beings and said to them, "I, Skan, and you, Inyan, Maka, and Wi, are four, but we are only one, and that one is Wakan Tanka, which no one can understand. Each of us is a part of Wakan Tanka which is the Great Incomprehensible. I, Skan, am the source of all power, and I shall give a rank and a domain to each of you. Wi shall be the chief of the Sacred Beings because I have placed him above all, even above the blue dome of myself. He shall govern the two times, Anpetu and Hanhepi, and all above the world is his domain.

"To myself I give the second rank, but because I am the source of all power and all spirit, I keep my authority over all, and my domain is everywhere.

"To Maka I give the third rank, and from her shall come all things upon the world. All lands except the mountains and high hills are her domain.

"To Inyan, from whom everything began, I give the fourth rank, and all mountains, rocks, and high hills are his domain. His color is yellow; the color of Maka is green; Wi's is the red of light; and mine is the blue of the dome above the world. So should the first Sacred Beings, who are four, yet one, be recognized by all."

Now the Sacred Beings were lonely and longed for companions. So Skan granted to each one the power to create for himself a companion.

Wi created a disk like himself, only more lovely, and named her Hanwi, the Moon. He made her less bright than himself so he could gaze upon her beauty. Together they governed the two times, daytime and nighttime.

Maka created a being of magical beauty, but gave her a part of her own ill-nature. She named her Unk, Passion. But she was so beautiful that Maka became jealous of her. They had a violent quarrel and Maka threw her into the waters and remained with no companion.

Skan created for his companion a being like himself, a spirit with no body, and he named him Tate, the Wind. Tate was his faithful servant and companion and traveled everywhere as Skan's messenger. Often he had to journey in the nighttime when all was darkness and he could see nothing. So Skan took from the waters a part of their spirit and out of it he made many tiny beings. These were the star people; and he placed them high above the blue dome of himself and gave them power to shine with a pale light that gives neither heat nor shadows. He commanded them to sleep while Wi was crossing the sky and to shine at night to give Tate light for his work, and to see all that happened on the world at night and to tell him what they saw. He made the North Star their chief, to direct them on their journey, for as yet there were no directions in the world.

Inyan remembered the trouble he caused himself in creating Maka, and decided to make a being unlike any other to be his helper. This was Wakinyan, the Thunderstorm, who is shapeless and terrifying to look at. He has two many-jointed wings which he can spread far out or make very small; he has neither legs nor feet, but huge talons that can pierce anything; he has no mouth, but a great beak with sharp teeth; he has no head, but a voice that is the thunder, and one eye whose glance is the lightning. Because of his terrible appearance, Skan told him he must hide when he did not intend to be seen, and so he made robes of clouds in which he wraps himself. Wakinyan is the opposite of all natural things, and his normal condition is anger. He loves opposition and contrariness. Inyan gave him a double nature so that he can appear as an amiable giant to those whom he wishes to please, and he gives growth and increase to all creatures. In this aspect, he is Heyoka, the Restorer.

Inyan gave Wakinyan for his home the level top of the high mountain at the edge of the world. There Wakinyan has a lodge with no roof and with striped walls, lined inside with sharp rocks, for he likes to rest on things that are hard and rough. From this lodge he flies over the world searching for evil things to destroy. Because Inyan cannot move, Wakinyan acts for him and carries out his wishes. He works with Tate to cleanse the world of filthy things.

Inyan was so pleased with his creature that he wished for offspring by him. So Wakinyan made a huge egg, and Inyan fertilized it. Wakinyan tumbled and tossed the egg, beat it with his wings, and roared at it with his thunder until the shell broke and a full-grown being came out of it, who had a strange shape. He was very wise, and Skan gave him a spirit and called him Ksa, Wisdom. The other Spirits laughed at his odd shape, but all except Unk liked him because he wished only to help and please them. He invented language and pleasant sounds; he told stories, and taught the Spirits games; and he gave names to all creatures and things.

Ksa was the first offspring of the Sacred Beings, and Skan gave him great powers but not the rank of the First Four. He was their counselor and gave them always good advice. Skan was so pleased with him that he decided he, too, would make an offspring for himself; so he created a daughter, and named her Woope, the Beautiful.

Woope is the loveliest and the most pleasing of all beings. Her father Skan made her the mediator among the Spirits, and between them and all things. He gave her the powers of a Spirit, and she became the Spirit of friendship and compassion, beauty, and happiness. The other Sacred Beings loved her and received her as their equal. Maka, since she had thrown out Unk and had no associate, begged Skan that Woope might be her companion, and Skan agreed, but decreed that Woope should never be Maka's servant nor subject to her will.

Now Unk, the Earth Spirit's rejected companion, was very beautiful, but she was vicious and longed for revenge against Maka who had cast her off into the waters. She went to Skan and wept for justice, and to make amends for the wrong that had been done to her, Skan gave her the waters as her domain, with powers to rule them as she wished, and the right to sit in the circle of the Sacred Beings. But Unk was not satisfied. She complained to Inyan of her loneliness, and her beauty made him forget his companion Wakinyan and fall in love with her. They had a son, who was the first creature to be born in the world, so Unk called him Tokapa, the First-born. He grew rapidly into a giant of great strength and evil disposition, but foolish. He went into rages for no reason and loved to destroy things, and in these rages he is known as Ibom, the Cyclone, who is the Spirit of disaster. Skan called him Iya, the Evil One; so Iya, Ibom, and Tokapa are the same evil Spirit. Unk was infatuated with him, and bore him a son, and because of this Inyan stayed with her no longer.

The son of Unk and Iya was beautiful and charming, but cunning and deceitful, and wanted only to do harm to others. His name was Gnaski, the Demon. Gnaski spared no one in his schemes to cause ridicule and to set the Spirits against each other, but because of his beauty and his cleverness and flattery, he managed to escape punishment and was welcome everywhere. He delighted in making use of the strength and foolishness of Iya, who was his father and also his brother, and contrived that Iya should suffer the blame for the evil tricks he persuaded him to play. He schemed without success how to bring ridicule on Ksa and Woope.

Now the first of all feasts was to be held in the assembly of the Sacred Beings, in the regions under the world where they met and where Skan announced his decrees. In the beginning there was no eating nor drinking, for the Spirits knew neither hunger nor thirst. But Hanwi, the Moon, said to Ksa, "Ksa gives pleasure with what can be seen and heard; can he not invent pleasures that can be tasted and smelled?"

Ksa replied, "I would do so with joy, but if I should create such things in the domain of any one of the Sacred Beings, the others would be jealous."

Woope said, "The regions under the world are not the domain of any Spirit; Ksa could create good things to taste and smell there, and invite the Spirits to enjoy them."

They asked Wakinyan, the Spirit of growth, to help them and he gave Woope a fine dust, and said, "Blow your breath upon this dust."

She did so and Wakinyan then gave the dust to Ksa, and said, "Go and plant this dust in the regions under the world."

When Ksa had planted it, it bore white fruits that had neither roots nor stems nor leaves nor flowers, and it had a delicious smell and taste.

Then Ksa made a lodge in the shape of a circle, with a door, because the world and the sky above it are both circles. To mark the place of honor he placed a seat at the back opposite the door. He borrowed heat from Wi and created a fire which he placed in the center of the circle. This was the first lodge and all lodges are made like it.

Woope made twelve bowls of earth for the guests, and cooking pots and spoons and ladles. Then she and Ksa gathered the white fruits, and placed some inside the lodge and some outside, and invited all the Spirits to come to the feast. Skan came with his companion Tate, Wi with Hanwi, and Maka came alone. Inyan came with Wakinyan in his friendly aspect as Heyoka. Iya and Gnaski came with their mother Unk. All wondered, for they did not know what a feast was, as they had never eaten nor drunk. But sly Gnaski whispered to Iya, "Go quickly and defile the store of white fruits outside the lodge, and we will make Woope and Ksa ridiculous," and Iya did so.

When all the Spirits had assembled, Ksa gave a seat to each. He gave the place of honor to Wi, as their chief, with Hanwi on his left and Skan on his right. Tate sat on Skan's right, with Maka next to him. Inyan was seated on Hanwi's left, with Wakinyan beside him, and Unk next. Iya and Gnaski were placed on opposite sides of the door, and Woope had a seat beside the fire at the center of the lodge. Ksa sat beside the door. But Wi rose and said, "The place of honor belongs to the Great Spirit, Skan, the source of all powers and wisdom." All the Spirits cried, "Good, let it be so," and Skan took the place of honor with his daughter Woope beside him, Tate on their right and Wi and Hanwi on their other side. This then was forever after the order in which the Sacred Beings sat.

When all had taken their appointed places, Woope took the fruits that were inside the lodge and put some on the fire to boil, some to toast, and of some she made a juice. Their odor filled the lodge and caused the Sacred Beings for the first time to feel hungry and thirsty. Then Woope filled each bowl with fruit and juice, and all ate and drank and were delighted, except Iya. He gulped down his food and asked rudely for more and more, and Woope served him until all the fruits in the lodge were gone. Then she took from those that were outside and served him again. He gulped them down and knew from their foul taste that they were from the store of fruits which he had defiled. They sickened him and he stormed at Woope for giving him filthy food.

But Skan knew what he had done, and said: "Because Iya defiled food intended for the Spirits, and is a glutton, and has spoken rudely to the daughter of the Great Spirit, he is not fit to sit with us and he shall go from us and sit no more with us. He shall be forever hungry with a hunger that cannot be satisfied, so he shall eat filth and his breath shall stink."

So Iya was sent away and never again sat with the Sacred Beings. Gnaski laughed, but Unk hid her face in shame over the disgrace of her son and lover.

Ksa said, "Woope has made a feast and served the Spirits until she is tired. The daughter of the Great Spirit should not have to work so hard at such tasks. It would be well if beings were created to serve the Spirits and do their will."

Then all the Spirits cried, "Let it be so," and Skan said, "Ho."

Skan took from Inyan something from which he created two sets of bones, one larger than the other. From Maka he took something from which he made flesh, and from the waters of Unk something from which he created blood. From the white fruits he formed entrails. He molded all together and made two images, one in the handsome form of Gnaski and one with the beauty of Woope. To each he gave a spirit like that of the Sacred Beings, but a little lower. To make this, he took from himself a *nagi*, a spirit that guides the conduct, and gave it to each of the two new beings to be their ghost or double. Then he gave to each the *nagila*, a particle of his own divine energy. He commanded Tate to breathe into each image a *niya*, the breath of life, and Wakinyan to give to each a *sicun*, the spirit which gives power to produce offspring, and to give health and growth. Wi warmed them; Ksa gave them intelligence; Hanwi gave them affection for each other, and Woope gave them longing and love for offspring.

Skan said to them: "Your names shall be Ate, Father, and Hunku, Mother, and you and your children shall be known as the Pte Oyate, the Buffalo People. You have been created to serve the Spirits, and this will make you happy. If you cease to serve them, you will be miserable, and your children after you. Your home shall be the regions under the world, and the white fruits your food. Ksa will instruct you how to live and how to serve the Sacred Beings."

Thus the Pte people were created, and they multiplied and obeyed the instructions of Ksa and Woope. They lived happily and became many families, and each family had a lodge. They felt neither heat nor cold, and the white fruits nourished them. These were the ancestors of mankind.

When the Spirits assembled under the world, the Pte served them all, and when Wi and Hanwi went there to rest in the night-time, they served them together. Hanwi began to consider them her servants, and spoke of them as her people, and Maka was jealous.

Gnaski saw this and schemed how to make use of it to cause trouble. He pretended to sympathize with Maka and urged her to complain to Skan. So when the Spirits feasted together again, Maka stood in their circle and said, "Oh Skan, Hanwi, who is not even one of the First Four, has her people who do her will. Give me servants also to help me make my domain green and beautiful, for it is now bare and ugly."

Gnaski thought that she would be ridiculed, and began to laugh, but Skan knew what he had planned. To foil his scheme he commanded Ksa, Woope, Tate, and Wakinyan to grant Maka's request and to work together to give her what she wished. They consulted together and created the green things, grass and plants and trees. Gnaski saw that his plot was frustrated, so he said to them, "It was I who first proposed this pleasure for Maka.

Let me at least help in the planting of these green things." They agreed and Gnaski spat on the plants they gave him and made them thorny or poisonous. He stole some of the white fruits from the regions under the world and planted them also, and they came up in one night but they had a foul odor and whoever ate them was sick. He breathed on the other plants so that they turned yellow and dried up.

Then Ksa said, "To live all must have blood. If water were given to the plants, perhaps Skan will make it into blood for them."

"My enemy Unk controls the waters," said Wakinyan. "She is envious of Maka and will not help to make her lands beautiful."

"Skan is just and will allow you to take what is needed from Unk so that the plants may grow," said Tate.

Wakinyan wrapped himself in robes of clouds and flew over the waters. He dipped the robes in water until they were soaked, and then he flew over the lands and squeezed his robes so that they spilled the water on the forest and the prairie, and the plants drew up the water and were nourished. Thus Wakinyan invented rain and ever since he moistens the land so that the plants grow.

Ksa returned to the circle of the Spirits and said, "The world was dry and barren, but now it is green and beautiful with the plants that grow from the ground. Many of them are good for food. Yet no sound is heard on the world except when a Spirit speaks or when Wakinyan brings rain. If there were creatures that made sounds, they would break the great silence and could eat the food that is ready for them."

"Tate gives life to all things which Wakinyan creates," said Skan.

Then Wakinyan took soft parts of the plants, and from these he created many kinds of small eggs, two of each kind. Tate breathed on them and Wi warmed them, and they hatched into insects of all sorts, two of each, male and female. Ksa taught each kind its language and showed them which plants were good for food and how to produce eggs and protect their offspring. Woope decorated them with many different colors. Maka promised to sustain them, but gave them as subjects to their creator Wakinyan.

Ksa went again to the circle of the Spirits and said: "Plants make the world beautiful, and insects inhabit it, but there is nothing of flesh and blood."

"Wakinyan may create whatever would be good," said Skan.

Wakinyan then took two eggs from each of the many kinds of insects and wrapped each egg with fruits. Tate breathed on them, and covered them with soil. Wi warmed them and they hatched, and became all the different kinds of reptiles, two of each kind, male and female. These became the subjects of Unk.

Then Wakinyan took other eggs, and gave them shells of different colors. Woope made nests of twigs and grass for the eggs. Wi warmed them and they hatched, producing creatures that were nearly naked and helpless, that cried for food. Woope fed them until she was exhausted, but still they cried and cried with hunger. Then Wakinyan commanded the insects to feed these creatures and they did so. They grew quickly and were soon covered with down, which became feathers, and Woope gave them different colors, some bright and some dull. Ksa taught them their languages and he taught them to fly.

Maka was delighted with them, and said, "I give to my companion, Woope, as her subjects, these most beautiful of Wakinyan's creations, which shall be called birds."

Then Unk was jealous, and said, "I was created to be your companion, and you withhold from me what should be mine."

Woope said to Unk, "Choose whichever of these birds you wish, and they shall be your subjects."

So Unk chose the cranes, the swans, the geese, the ducks, and the snipes.

All the Spirits saw that the creations of Wakinyan were good. But Inyan stood in the circle of the Spirits and said, "Long ago, I thought I would bring pleasure to myself by making the first creation. This was Maka. She was never satisfied, and her complaints and demands have brought about all the other creations. Because of her, all creatures exist and are pleasing to all, but she still has none to serve her and be subject to her. I beg that Skan will make creatures a little inferior to the Pte people who will be subjects of Maka and do what she wishes."

All the Spirits said, "Let it be so," and Skan said, "Ho."

Skan assembled all the Spirits and all the creatures that breathed on the world, and in their presence he created the animals. He took clay from the ground, and a certain substance from all the creatures, and mixed them. He commanded the Spirits to mold shapes with four limbs and no wings.

Wi and Hanwi molded shapes with horns and hooves. Maka and Woope molded shapes with claws and blunt teeth. Inyan and Wakinyan molded shapes with claws and pointed teeth. But Unk defied Skan's command and molded shapes without limbs.

Skan told Wakinyan to clothe all these shapes. He covered some with coarse hair, some with fine hair, some with fur, and some with a mixture of these things. But when he came to the shapes molded by Unk, she glared at him. So he clothed these shapes with slime or with scales.

Then Skan told Wi to warm them, and he did so; but when he came to the ones covered with slime and scales, Unk glared at him. So he turned away and they remained cold. And Skan said, "Because Unk has disobeyed my command and refused the help that was offered, the creatures she has shaped shall be cold as long as they live."

Then he gave each shape a spirit so that each became a living thing, and told Ksa to teach them and give them names. Ksa taught them their languages and how they were to live, and told them they were the animals, created to live on the earth and be the servants of Maka. But when he came to the ones shaped by Unk, he was puzzled, for they could not move on the ground because they had no limbs. So he told them, "You must live in the waters, and make no sound, so you need no language. You are the fishes and you shall be the subjects of Unk."

So the animals were created on the ground and the fishes in the waters. But Unk was not satisfied with the fishes and some of the birds, and complained that she had too little. So Maka said, "Of all those in my domain, choose what you desire and they shall be yours." Unk chose the reptiles, and so they became her subjects.

One of the reptiles was named Unhcegi. He was huge, with four feet and three toes on each foot, and on each toe a sharp hoof with which he could cut and tear. When he was angry his bellow was like the thunder of Wakinyan. Unk looked on him with lust and took him for her mate. She bore him offspring that were shaped like huge lizards. They had rows of tusks and cutting teeth, and enormous tails with which they could strike blows that could shatter rocks. Each had four horns that they could extend or pull in. They were called the Unktehi, the Monsters, and even Unk was afraid of them.

Gnaski advised his mother to create exceedingly small creatures that would live in the waters, so small that they would be swallowed by other creatures drinking the water and in whose bodies they could then create pain and sickness. Unk created them and named them the Mini Watu, and they live in foul and stagnant water. Wakinyan destroys them whenever he can, but he is forbidden to enter the waters so most of them are safe from him. Then Unk created another creature that has a shell of bone, a head like a bird, a beak without teeth, and strong legs that can walk on land or swim in the water. She named it Keya, the Turtle, and it was her servant and obeyed her commands. Gnaski made trouble between Keya and Iya so that they fought, and Wakinyan, who was Iya's enemy, watched to see if he could make use of this. He asked Keya, "What are your duties?"

Keya said, "I do what I am bidden."

"Since you can live and breathe in the waters which I cannot enter, you can help me in my work of cleaning the world by destroying the Mini Watu. If you do this, I will not be your enemy, even though you belong to Unk's domain," said Wakinyan.

Keya agreed, and Wakinyan promised him many offspring. This is why an image of Keya placed on a baby's navel protects it from colic and the bowel diseases caused by the Mini Watu.

When the Sacred Beings came together to feast and take counsel, Unk stood before them and said, "I am the only one of all the ruling Spirits who has not been given the power to create a companion. So I have chosen Unhcegi as my companion and demand that you accept him."

Skan said, "You were created as a companion; but because Maka cast you out, I was sorry for you and raised you above the others. If you claim more for yourself, you will make trouble for all. Let Unhcegi be advised by Ksa and he may do well."

"My companion shall not be advised by the deformed son of my enemy Wakinyan," said Unk. "I and my sons laugh at Ksa's ridiculous shape, and we will advise Unhcegi."

"Then he will have no favor with the First Four and their Circle," said Skan.

"I ask no favors. I will take what I should have," said Unk.

"Then others will take from you what they wish," said Skan.

"I shall defend with force what I have," cried Unk. "Ibom, my son, and Unhcegi my companion can withstand even Wakinyan. I challenge the Sacred Beings!"

"You separate yourself from us," said Skan. "Go from our circle and do not come to it again!"

"I leave you gladly!" shrieked Unk in a rage. "My own powers are enough for me! I shall neither ask nor give any favors. My pleasure will be in deceiving others and in nurturing lust and folly."

She called her sons Iya and Gnaski, her spouse Unhcegi and his offspring the Unktehi, and said to them, "I am a Spirit and my children are the offspring of a Spirit and Unhcegi is a Spirit's companion. Since we are banished from the circle of the Sacred Beings, I will make one of my own, and all of you shall have seats in my circle. Unhcegi shall be on my right and Iya on my left. Gnaski, you shall be warden and sit by the door. The Unktehi shall sit on either side. My circle is the enemy of the circle of the Sacred Beings, and we will find out how to prevent their plans from succeeding. I depend on the strength of Iya and Unhcegi to defeat Wakinyan and on the cunning of Gnaski to outwit Ksa. We have only Skan to fear, for he is beyond our power."

"I am the largest, and I shall serve you with all my strength," said Iya.

"Dear mother," said Gnaski, "I drew deceit from your breasts; I inherited cruelty and lust from my parents. I respect no one, and I do not fear Skan since he allowed me to be your son. These are my qualities, and with them I shall serve you when it gives me pleasure."

This is how the circle of evil Spirits was formed, and Unk commanded them to make trouble.

"Most lovable mother, what would please you most?" asked Gnaski.

"It would please me if Ksa were made ridiculous," said Unk.

"Your wish must be obeyed," said Gnaski.

He disguised himself to look exactly like Ksa, and walked among the creatures on the world. He amused them with funny tricks, and he imitated the wise sayings of Ksa in such a way that they laughed. They all gathered about him, laughing more and more as he made fun of everything. Maka and Woope came to find out what was going on, and they also laughed, thinking it was Ksa.

Maka said, "Ksa, your humor is pleasing, and you are giving much enjoyment with it which is like wisdom. When you teach like this, you should be called Ksapela, Little Wisdom."

"I am indeed Ksapela, the other aspect of Ksa," said Gnaski. "I bring cheer into the gloom of wisdom."

"You are welcome in my domain," said Maka. "You may come and go as you wish."

Afterwards, Ksa himself came to visit the creatures. They gathered around him and he spoke words of wisdom to them. A grasshopper said, "Say something funny."

"If you feed on fun, you will be hungry," said Ksa.

"If you feed on wise words, you will be hungry," said an owl. Ksa was confused and the creatures laughed.

"Do some funny dances," croaked a frog.

"His shape is funny because he was hatched from a queer egg," buzzed a fly.

"Can you fly?" screamed an eagle.

"Can you crawl?" whispered an ant.

"Show me how to swim," said the duck.

"Let's see you hop," said the toad.

Ksa was sad because they all ridiculed him, and he went away. Gnaski was watching, and he followed him and said, "Fun has outwitted wisdom. Wisdom and fun combined could rule the world."

"Then wisdom would be banished from the circle of the Sacred Beings," said Ksa.

Gnaski said, "You are only their doorkeeper, and they give you very little respect. My mother also was banished from their circle and created her own. You and I working together could control her circle and have greater power than anyone except Skan." Ksa was troubled and went to find Maka and Woope; but when he spoke to them wisely, they laughed. Ksa was astonished.

Woope said, "We laugh because what you said reminded us of the jokes told by your other part, Ksapela."

"Ksapela is not my other part," said Ksa. "He is my opposite. He is folly."

"A little folly gives more pleasure," said Maka.

Meanwhile Gnaski returned to his mother's circle and boasted of how he had made Ksa ridiculous. Unk was pleased, but then he mocked her also, and the others around her.

"Are you not one of us?" asked Unk.

"This circle delights me," said Gnaski. "This huge reptile Unhcegi takes the place in your affections of my father Iya, the huge son of a Spirit. This must please my father, and you must be very happy for when one of them is absent you can make love with the other."

Iya and Unhcegi glared at each other, and Unk cried, "Go from us, Gnaski!"

"Where shall I go, my honored mother?" asked Gnaski.

"You are like the Pte people. Go to them," said Unk.

Tate
and
Ite

The Pte lived together in the regions under the world, and served the Sacred Beings. Ate ruled them as a father, and they obeyed him. They were many, old and young, and they revered their forebears and loved their children and their kindred. The wisest of them all was Wazi, and his wife Wakanka was a wise woman who could see into the future.

Skan wished to know more of what went on among them, so he commanded his companion Tate to take on the form of a man and to go and live among them for a time. So Tate appeared among the Pte as a robust stranger in his prime, and the people were curious and did not know whether to accept him or not. Ate heard them and said, "A stranger is a friend until he is proven an enemy. He is a guest while he is with us, and if he stays with us, he is *kola*, a comrade."

The people shouted and said, "Ksa has spoken through the mouth of our father Ate." Then Tate was welcomed by all and they called him Kola. Wazi said to him, "Kola, live with me in the lodge of Wakanka, and you shall be like our son."

"While I am with the Pte, I shall live as the son of Wakanka according to the customs of the people," said Kola.

Wazi and Wakanka had a daughter called Ite, who was the most beautiful of all women. She had built no lodge of her own. She looked in the faces of many young men, and smiled. But she sat with none of them before her mother's fire, though many came to do so. Wazi and Kola often sat together in the lodge of Wakanka and talked, and Kola often looked at Ite. He thought she became more and more beautiful. Wakanka saw this and said to Ite, "Daughter, Kola's thoughts are of you. He is more than a man. There will be much pleasure in the lodge he lives in."

Ite said, "Mother, let us prepare materials, for I would like to have a lodge of my own."

One day Kola sat in the lodge of Wakanka with Wazi, and Ite also was there. Kola said, "I am going back to where I came from, but if the Sacred Beings will permit, I will return to live with the Pte people. If I do, I want to sit in the lodge of your daughter Ite.

If she will lead me through her door, I shall try to make her happy."

Ite cut a lock of her hair and gave it to him, saying, "That you may not forget."

Tate appeared before Skan and said, "I lived with the Pte people as a man. They have multiplied and are many. They are happy living in the regions under the world and serving the gods. But Ate and Hunku are withered and their *nagi* are feeble. Wazi is the wisest of all men and the leader of the Pte people, and he should be the next chief after Ate, whose *nagi* struggles to remain in his body and who longs to have another take his place. Wazi's wife, Wakanka, is the wisest of women and a seer; she would be of great help to him. Their daughter Ite is the most beautiful and lovely of womankind.

"I learned to love this Ite in a way that Spirits cannot feel, and she would share her lodge with me. In order to live with her, I would give up my powers as a Spirit and become a man. But if it is your will, I will faithfully be your companion."

Skan said, "Your wish is granted. You may return to the Pte as a man, and live with Ite until her offspring leave your lodge. Your seat in the circle of the Sacred Beings shall be kept for your return. Meanwhile, my daughter Woope shall be my companion. While you are living as a man, my will is that you feel to the utmost all the human passions, for as these sway you, so they shall temper my judgments."

So Tate returned as Kola to the lodge of Wakanka.

Now when Gnaski was dismissed by Unk to go and spread trouble among the Pte, he persuaded Iya, his giant father-brother, to go with him, promising him to satisfy his insatiable hunger with the food of the Spirits, the white fruits that grew in the regions under the world and nourished the Pte people also. Gnaski appeared among the people in his role of Ksapela, but disguised as a handsome young man. He entertained them with tricks and games, and distracted their attention so that they forgot to guard the field where the white fruits grew. While Gnaski amused them, Iya gorged himself on the fruits and stole all that he could not eat; so when the people went to gather some, they found none at all. They returned in dismay and told what had happened, but they couldn't agree about who was to blame.

"Soon the Spirits will come for their feast. What shall we say to them?" said Wazi.

"Tell them that you guarded the fruits, but they were stolen," said Ksapela. "I will search for the thief, and if I find him you may have vengeance."

"Ksa taught us nothing of vengeance. What is it?" said the people.

"It is the justice of repayment for injury or insult. One who causes pain or grief is repaid by suffering," said Ksapela.

Ate was feeble and stayed in his lodge, but he heard the clamor and was told what had happened. Then he said, "Now, my *nagi*, go from me, for my children are foolish and I would not see the frown of the Great Spirit."

His *nagi* went from him and he was cold and lifeless, and the *nagi* of Hunku departed also. But their spirits lingered for they had no place to go.

When the Sacred Beings assembled for their feast, Wazi said, "The people wish to serve you but the food has been stolen."

"How did this happen?" said Skan.

"Ksapela distracted them and the people forgot their duty," said Wazi. "Now they are full of remorse and they are hungry. Also they mourn because the *nagi* of Ate and Hunku have left their bodies; but their spirits linger near."

"Ate's spirit always counseled him wisely. It may advise his children," said Skan. "Ksa will teach you how to seek this advice."

Ksa stood before the people and said, "Choose one whom I will prepare to receive a message from the spirit of your father Ate."

The people chose Wazi, and Ksa said to him, "By preparing you to receive the message of a Spirit, I make you a holy man, through whom the Spirits will speak to the people and tell them what they wish. If you use deceit and trickery, the Sacred Beings will not know you and your people will cast you out.

"Sit with your head bowed, and vow to speak truly of the messages you receive from the Spirits."

Wazi did so. Then Ksa told the people to pass by Wazi and one by one to place their hands on his head and vow to receive his words as the will of the Sacred Beings; and the people obeyed.

Ksa said to Wazi, "Cleanse your body and go alone to a place where there is no other living thing. Stay there without eating or drinking, meditating on the message you wish to receive, until it comes to you. Then return and tell your people. If one of the Spirits wishes to speak through you, this message will come to you as in a dream."

Then Ksa said to the people, "The Sacred Beings will not talk directly with you any more as they have done, but will send you messages through your holy men. Continue to serve them and all will be well with you.

"Take the bodies of Ate and Hunku and place them on a hill. Put beside them all that they had when they were alive, and bring gifts also and put them beside them. Do this whenever the *nagi* departs from one of your people, for the *sicun* will return from whence it came, but the ghost, the *nagi*, will appear before the Great Spirit and tell about how the spirit, the *nagila*, conducted itself in life. Skan will then judge whether it is worthy to go on the spirit road to the spirit world and to live there forever in happiness and pleasure. If so, the spirit part of all the things you place beside the body will go with the *nagila* and serve it in that other world."

Then the people were glad and no longer afraid.

Wazi went away as Ksa told him and fasted alone. He heard the command that each of the people stand up before all the others and confess his folly, and he brought the message back to the people. They grumbled because he didn't promise them food. Kola stood before them and said, "You are hungry and you suffer because of your folly. How much worse will it be for you if you forget the vow you made when you laid your hands on Wazi's head?"

Then they were ashamed, and all day and into the night they all stood up one by one and confessed their fault. Then they slept and when it was morning, they looked and saw an abundance of the white fruits.

Often Kola sat in the lodge of Wakanka and talked with her and with Wazi. Ite listened and smiled at him, but she looked also at other men and Kola saw this and was sad. Ksapela also came to the lodge of Wakanka, and he flattered her and Wazi, telling them that they were wiser and greater than all others. He flattered Ite also and told her that she was so beautiful that she should sit with the Spirits rather than serve them at their feasts. He told her that he came from a realm where his mother was the ruler, and that he was searching for a companion worthy of his high position.

Ite asked her mother to look into the future and tell her about Ksapela.

"He also is more than a man," said Wakanka. "But he makes people happy only for selfish reasons."

"Which shall I choose, Ksapela or Kola?" asked Ite.

"One of these two will sit at the place of honor in your lodge, but I cannot tell which one," said Wakanka. "Because of you, your parents shall be like the Spirits. Try to choose the one who will help you most."

"Ksapela is very handsome," said Ite.

Kola watched and was sad, and he stopped visiting Wakanka's lodge. After some time that he had not come, Ite said to her mother, "Kola hates me and I hate him. Bring me my most beautiful clothing and ornaments. I will put them on and go and scorn him as he scorns me."

She made herself beautiful and went toward Kola. He looked at her with longing, but she gazed over his head and he turned his face from her. Again she passed him and she looked at him but he stood with downcast eyes. The third time she approached and their glances met. She stood before him and said, "My father is grieved by your absence from our lodge. If I am an offense to your sight, I will go away."

Then Kola smiled and said, "I will go with you to your mother's lodge, but only if you lead me through the door." Ite took him by the hand and together they went to Wakanka's lodge. Ite said to her parents, "I have found my man." Wakanka seated Kola in the place of honor, and prepared a feast.

Ksapela knew all that was going on. He entered Wakanka's lodge and said, "I would wish to stay here among the Pte people, but my mother has summoned me and I must go. Beautiful Ite, come with me and our lives will be happy and full of pleasure."

"I am Kola's woman," said Ite.

Ksapela pretended to be astonished and heartbroken, and begged as a last favor before he left that Ite should walk a little way with him to soften his sorrow with the memory of a kind parting. In his happiness, Kola agreed to this, but told Ite not to go far. The two left the lodge, but Wakanka sat with bowed head, and after they had been gone a little time, she cried out that Ite was in danger, and told Wazi and Kola to hurry after her. As they went, Kola prayed to Skan, saying, "Oh Great Spirit, send help if Ite is in danger; I, your comrade, ask it."

Now Ksapela had used all his charm and magical tricks to entertain Ite and without thinking she had let him lead her far from her mother's lodge; but suddenly she remembered and wished to go back. Ksapela again begged her to go on with him but she refused. He seized her by the arm and shouted, "Ho, Iya!" And immediately the giant Iya appeared from his hiding place, and Ksapela cried, "You will go with me or this giant will take you captive!"

"Pity my weakness!" cried Ite.

"I know nothing of pity," said Ksapela.

"Gnaski, you have been taking your pleasure with this beautiful woman, while I starved," roared Iya. "Give her to me!"

"Ksapela, save me!" shrieked Ite. "Think of your mother!"

"He is not Ksapela, he is Gnaski the demon, my brother and son, and I am Iya. Our mother is Unk, and she will be happy to see what we make of you!" yelled Iya. He seized her in his arms, and she wept and cried out for Kola to come and help her. At that moment Kola and Wazi appeared running, and Kola leapt at Iya, but Iya with one blow of his huge hand knocked him senseless. Then thunder sounded from above, and Wakinyan was there flashing his lightning. He struck Iya down, and Gnaski fled and hid in a cave.

Wazi and Ite carried Kola to Wakanka's lodge, and when he opened his eyes, his head was in Ite's lap.

"I had a terrible dream," he said.

"My dreams have come true," Ite said.

"When you prayed to the Great Spirit as we went in search of Ite, you called him comrade," said Wazi. "Are you Tate, the comrade of Skan?"

"I was Tate," said Kola.

Wakanka bowed her head. "I foresaw that my daughter would marry a Spirit," she said.

Wakanka and Ite made a new lodge near the lodge of Wakanka. When it was done, Ite led Kola by the hand through the door of the new lodge and seated him in the place of honor, and sat beside the fireplace at the center of the lodge. Thus was established the family of Kola.

Ite and Kola lived together happily, and she bore him four sons at one birth, so that all the people knew that they were more than human. Wazi and Wakanka went to sing and pray over the babies; Wakanka sang:

"My husband is a holy man.
I am a wise woman and a seer.

My daughter is the wife of a Spirit.
My grandchildren are *wakan*.
They shall be as *Wakan Tanka*."

Wazi wished for them that they would become a pride to their parents. Wakanka wished that her daughter should become ever more beautiful and that her offspring should be as Spirits, so that they and their parents should never be forgotten.

Then they named the four babies, the first-born Yata, the second Eya, the third Yanpa, and the last Okaga. As they named Yata he scowled at them. As they named Eya he yawned and waved his arms. As they named Yanpa he slept. And as they named Okaga he smiled and laughed. Then Wakanka said that as they were when they were named, so should they be for all time.

Gnaski and Iya had returned to the realm of their mother Unk. She was angry because they had failed to capture Ite, but Gnaski only laughed and mocked her.

"Dear mother, wherever I am and whatever I do, I am spreading your domain," he said. "I have already sowed the seeds of discord among the Pte people, and sooner or later I shall bring about the downfall of Ksa himself. But first I shall see what can be done among the insects and the animals, and find some way of annoying Maka."

Gnaski worked on the stupid and bad-tempered Iya to feed his anger against Wakinyan for rescuing Ite from him, and brought about furious battles between the two. Wakinyan had not forgotten his enmity against Unk and her offspring since she had long ago seduced his companion Inyan, and gladly sought to destroy Iya. Gnaski contrived that their most terrible battles should be in the domain of Maka, in order to trouble her. The clouds swirled, the lightning flashed, Wakinyan thundered and Iya roared as Ibom, the Cyclone; but because Inyan had produced them both, neither could ever destroy the other, but Iya was always defeated and driven back to his mother's domain, where Wakinyan could not follow him. But Gnaski was pleased because parts of Maka's region were torn and damaged and her trees uprooted, except for the sacred cedar trees which were protected by Skan.

Gnaski taught many of the insects to suck blood and bother the animals, and even afflicted his mother's spouse Unhcegi with fleas. Then he went to spread strife among the animals. He disguised himself as Ksapela and they made him welcome. First he stayed with the hoofed people. He talked with an old moose, and said to him: "I advise you not to choose a chief, but if you insist on doing so, you with your impressive shape and antlers should be chosen chief instead of the bear."

"I know nothing about the animals choosing a chief," said the moose.

"Perhaps the bear has hidden his ambitious plans from you for fear you might win more followers than he," said Ksapela.

The moose discussed the matter with the elders of the hoofed beings and they declared that he should be chosen chief. Ksapela stayed next with the animals with claws, and talked with the bear.

"The moose is plotting to be chosen chief of all animals, but surely it should be you who are so strong and wise," he said to the bear.

The bear went at once to confer with the elders of the clawed beings and they declared that he should be chosen chief. Ksapela went next among the diggers, and said to them, "A moose and a bear are each plotting to become chief of all the animals. My advice is that you do not choose a chief, but if you must choose, consider well; for the diggers and builders outnumber all the other animals and could decide which should be chief. So choose the one that will be best for you, and then convince the builders to agree with you."

"Which would be best for us?" asked the prairie dog.

"Those having claws could compel you to do what they wish, but those having hoofs can do you little harm," said Ksapela.

The diggers immediately had a conference and decided that they would oppose any of those with claws. Ksapela then went to the community of the builders, and said to them: "A moose and a bear are each plotting to become chief of all the animals. My advice is that you do not choose a chief; but the hoofs and the diggers have decided that the moose shall be chief. You have not been consulted and they think they can control you. I only tell you this to warn you of the danger which threatens you."

Immediately the builders had a conference and decided their only safety was in choosing the bear. When the diggers sent an envoy to consult with the builders and to speak for the moose, there was an uproar and the envoy was driven away. The birds took sides, some for the bear and some for the moose. Soon there was such a hubbub of lauding and berating, accusing and denying, that Ksa came among the animals to try and make peace. He spoke words of wisdom to them and begged them to give up the folly of choosing a chief and to return to the peaceful communities they had had before.

"Can we not manage our own affairs, and decide to better ourselves?" the animals demanded.

"Choose as you desire, but I warn you that you will repent of your folly," answered Ksa.

Gnaski mingled with the animals and suggested that they choose two to fight a battle as champions for the two who were contestants for chief, and that the chief be decided accordingly. So a porcupine and a skunk were chosen. Ksa again protested, but the animals jeered at him and went on with their preparations for the battle. A magpie, a rabbit, an antelope, and an owl were chosen as judges. The skunk and the porcupine approached each other warily, and then turned and backed toward each other, the porcupine preparing to strike with his tail and the skunk with his stink. The porcupine looked over his shoulder before striking, and the skunk discharged his stink full in his face. At the same moment he was struck by the porcupine's tail and as the quills pierced him, he squalled and fled, and the porcupine gagged, coughed, retched, and fled also. All the other animals ran before them. No one was left but the judges.

The magpie said, "I concluded my verdict when the combatants were chosen."

"I agree with you," said the rabbit.

"We should deliberate. What was it we were to decide?" said the owl.

"I will decide as the rest of you do," said the antelope.

"Let us give our report," said the magpie. Returning to where the other animals had gathered, he announced, "Considering the facts, the porcupine was the winner; but for other reasons, we decide in favor of the skunk."

All the animals acclaimed this as just, and returned home.

"For whom was the skunk the champion?" asked Ksa. No one knew. He asked the skunk, "For whom did you fight?"

"For myself," said the skunk.

Then Ksa said, "On the earth, folly has overpowered wisdom."

When the Spirits next sat together, they laughed at the way the animals had acted. Hanwi made fun of Ksa for not having been able to stop them, and Ksa was ashamed and sad.

Gnaski came to him and said, "You are wisdom, yet all laugh at you. I am folly, but all laugh with me. Why is this so? Do you fear to appear in any other shape than the queer one you wear? Why should not wisdom also be beautiful? You can help me to make wisdom cheerful and attractive. Were we together, all would laugh with us. Let us associate, and our power will be greater than that of any but Skan."

"I will associate with you, but only as an experiment that I may stop if I wish," said Ksa.

"We must appear together, young and handsome, and so much

alike that no one can tell one from the other," said Gnaski.

Then the two stood together and the people marveled because they could not distinguish one from the other.

"How can we know which is Ksa and which is Ksapela?" they asked.

In his new guise, Ksa went to the feast of the Spirits and sat in their circle, and all but Skan challenged him as a stranger. Ksa said, "I am Ksa, and I have assumed this form in order to be more acceptable in the sight of all."

"My son, would you shame me by disguising the shape I gave you?" said Wakinyan.

Ksa said, "You brought me forth in a shape that caused ridicule. Laughter at my appearance has always been grievous to me. The Great Spirit granted the powers I have, and by these powers I have assumed this form."

Woope said, "Whatever your form, it is because of your words and deeds that I have been your companion."

"But with your present appearance, wisdom is more attractive," said Hanwi.

After a little, Ksa left the lodge, and while he was gone Gnaski as Ksapela came in his place and sat in his seat. Hanwi was charmed by his talk, and even Woope thought that it was Ksa, though she was surprised by the way he spoke. But Skan looked at him and Gnaski rose in fear and left the lodge.

Soon Ksa entered and sat down, and Skan said, "When wisdom bargains with folly, folly sits in the seat of wisdom. In your bargain with Gnaski, you both assumed the guise of youths so alike as to deceive even the Spirits. Through your act, the demon Gnaski sat in the circle of the Sacred Beings and all were deceived, except me. The bonds of your bargain shall bind you forever, and only with great difficulty shall you be able to know what is wise and what is foolish."

Then Skan called Wazi to appear before the Sacred Beings and said to him, "Wazi, it is by the choice of the people that you are a holy man and their chief. Now the Spirit of wisdom and the demon of folly are so alike that they can be distinguished only with great care. As you listen to Ksa or to Gnaski, so shall be the welfare of your people."

Ksa was troubled and he said to Ksapela, "You have brought only evil to me. I have suffered much humiliation because of you."

Ksapela said, "Master, it grieves me that others make sport of you. Even that which you do for the good of others is received with reprimands or ridicule. If the Spirits could be made to feel the injustice done you, then none would make sport of you."

Ksa listened, and Ksapela persuaded him to try a trick. He was to cause a young man of the Pte people to become foolish like a clown so that all would laugh at him. Then he would say that the young man was possessed by *iktomi*, the spider, and that he, Ksa, would cure him. He was to take a spider web and hide the *iktomi* in his hand, and putting bits of the web in the young man's nostrils he would pretend to catch the *iktomi* in his hand when the young man sneezed. Ksa did this, and the young man was so foolish that even the Spirits laughed at him. Then Ksa pretended to catch the *iktomi*, and caused the young man to regain his senses.

But Skan said, "Ksa has become Iktomi the spider, and his name shall no longer be Ksa but Iktomi."

So Ksa-Iktomi sat no more in the circle of the Sacred Beings, and because of his tricks he was shunned by every living being. He became full of hatred and looked about for any harm he could do.

Wazi was the holy man and chief of the Pte, but he was not satisfied, for he wished for the powers of the Spirits, and his wife Wakanka also wished for more and more power and honors.

Iktomi knew that Wazi wished for such powers and he said to Wazi, "If you will help me to cause others to be laughed at, I will give you the powers you wish for."

Wazi was afraid to help Iktomi with his schemes, but Wakanka urged him to agree to do as Iktomi wished, and Wazi said to Iktomi, "First give us the powers, and if we can do as the Spirits do, then we will help you as you wish."

Iktomi promised to do so and went from the lodge, but he hid near and heard Wakanka say to Wazi, "If we get these powers, they cannot be taken away from us except by Skan, and then we will help Iktomi only when we wish to do so."

Iktomi smiled and said, "This woman thinks she can deceive me because she is a wise woman." He returned to their lodge with roots and herbs which he powdered and mixed together, singing strange songs and saying strange words. He divided the mixture into parts and with each part he put hair from a wolf, a feather from a hawk, and a spider. He then made two bags, one shaped like a turtle and the other like a lizard. He put one portion of the mixture in each bag and breathed on them. He gave the bag shaped like a turtle to Wazi and that like a lizard to Wakanka, and said to them, "You must keep these bags as sacred things, for they have all the power that I have as a Spirit. When you wish to do a mysterious thing, breathe on them and ask them to help you and they will do it. When you have proved that you have my powers, tell me."

He often visited them and talked to them of the beauty of their daughter, and he told them that by means of the bags he had given them, they could make a charm that would cause the one to wear it to become more beautiful each night. He talked with Ite and praised her beauty, saying that she was almost as beautiful as Hanwi, the companion of Wi, chief of the Sacred Ones. He said to her, "You are the wife of a Spirit and the mother of Spirits, and you ought to have a seat with the Sacred Beings."

Ite told her mother what Iktomi had said to her and Wakanka said, "As a wise woman, I can foretell that you will sit beside the chief of the Spirits." So Wazi and Wakanka gave Ite the charm they had made and she grew more beautiful each night.

Then Iktomi said to Ite, "Wi is weary of Hanwi, and if another as beautiful as she would appear before him, he would take her also as a companion. You grow more beautiful each night and soon you will be more beautiful than Hanwi."

Ite told this to her mother and she said, "When you have sat beside the chief of the Spirits, you and your mother and your father will be spoken of after all of mankind who now live have been long forgotten."

Each night the Sacred Beings came together at the camp of the people under the world and had their feasts there. Here Iktomi said to Wi, "Ite, the daughter of the chief of the people, is the wife of a Spirit and the mother of Spirits. She should be honored above other women, but the Spirits do not honor her as she deserves. If you would honor her, then others would give her her due."

Wi said, "This is a small thing but I will do it."

Iktomi then said to Wazi and Wakanka, "Your daughter does not receive from the Spirits the honor that is due her, but if you will walk with her before Wi, he will honor her as should be done and then all others will do so."

They walked with their daughter before the face of Wi and he saw that she was very beautiful. He smiled upon her and spoke to her. Then all were very friendly to her.

Tate, her husband, was very happy but she was vain and flouted him. She neglected his children and his lodge and often walked before Wi and Wi often spoke to her. He bid her to the feast of the Sacred Beings and Iktomi heard him do so. Iktomi said to Ite, "If you sit beside Wi, he will take you for his companion. Go early to the feast and sit on the seat of Hanwi."

She went early and sat on the seat of Hanwi, and Wi came and looked on her beauty and he did not reprove her. Hanwi came and saw Ite sitting on her seat and she saw that Wi did not reprove her.

Hanwi stood and covered her face; for she was shamed before

the people and they laughed at her. She went and stood before Skan and he said, "Why does the most beautiful of the Spirits cover her face?"

She replied, "A woman sits on my seat at the feast of the Sacred Beings and Wi does not reprove her. I am shamed before the people and they laugh at me. Therefore I cover my face."

Skan said to Wi, "Why have you permitted a woman to sit on the seat of Hanwi?"

Wi replied, "This woman is the wife of a Spirit and the mother of Spirits and should be honored above all other women. As chief of the Sacred Beings, I would honor her as she deserves so that others would do so. I bid her to the feast. She sat on the seat of Hanwi and I looked on her beauty and it caused me to forget my companion."

Skan said to Ite, "Woman, why did you sit on the seat of Hanwi?"

She replied, "My father and my mother caused me to grow more beautiful each night and my mother foretold that I should sit beside the chief of the Spirits. Iktomi told me that Wi wished for another companion and that if one as beautiful as Hanwi appeared before him, he would take her to be with him. He told me that I was more beautiful than Hanwi and as Wi had bidden me to the feast, I should go early and sit on her seat."

Skan said to Wakanka, "Wise woman, why did you foretell to your daughter that she would sit beside the chief of the Spirits?"

Wakanka replied, "I foresaw that she would do so but I did not know that she would sit on the seat of Hanwi. Iktomi gave to me and to my husband the power to do as the Spirits do; and by this power we thought to avoid harm caused by our daughter sitting with the Sacred Beings."

Skan said to Wazi, "Why did you cause your daughter to grow more beautiful and walk with her before the face of Wi?"

Wazi replied, "I thought that with the power given to me by Iktomi, I would fit my daughter for a place with her husband and her children among the Spirits. I walked with her before the face of Wi to learn if the chief of the Spirits would honor her as she should be honored."

Skan said to Iktomi, "Why have you schemed to cause the people to laugh at Hanwi?"

Iktomi replied, "I am the first-born son of Inyan, the oldest of the Sacred Beings and the ancestor of all things, and I should be regarded as a Sacred Being. But because I was born of Wakinyan, he who has no shape, my shape is queer and all regard me as a clown. What I do to please others is made a sport. I am weary of being the sport of the Spirits and of mankind. Now I shall laugh and I shall cause others to be laughed at, and by my powers as a Spirit I will spare none. I have brought shame on the chief of the Sacred Beings and the chief of the people, on the most beautiful of the Sacred Beings and the most beautiful of women, and the people have laughed at them. Let all who have laughed at me beware, for I will cause them to be laughed at."

Then Skan said, "Each of you who have helped in this scheme to cause Hanwi to be laughed at and to cover her face in shame, hear what shall be your punishment.

"Wi, because you let the beauty of a woman make you forget your companion, Hanwi, she shall abide with you no more. From now and forever, you and she shall journey far apart. When she is nearest to you, she shall hide her face from you and only uncover it when she is farthest from you. You will continue to govern the two times, the day and the night; but she shall also govern a time and it shall be longer than either the day or the night. It shall be from when she is nearest to you until she goes farthest from you and returns again near to you. That all may know that it is her time, it shall be called a moon.

"Ite, because you flouted your husband and neglected your children, you shall go upon the world and wander there until there is a fourth time. Your unborn child shall come before its time and will always be little. He shall abide with his father and be known as his little son. Because you were so vain of your beauty that you dared to sit on the seat of Hanwi and schemed to take her place as the companion of Wi, you shall remain the most beautiful of women but you shall have another face, and it shall be so horrible that whosoever looks upon it shall detest you. Because you have sat on the seat of a Sacred Being, you shall live forever and shall be known as Anog Ite, the Two-faced or the Double Woman.

"Wakanka, with your foreknowing as a wise woman, you caused your daughter to offend Tate and make Hanwi ashamed. You shall go and abide alone upon the world until there is a fourth time. Because of the power that Iktomi has given you, you shall live forever and shall be known as Wakanka, the Old Woman, the Witch.

"Wazi, because you bargained with Iktomi to help him in making others ashamed, and with the power you received from him you helped in making Hanwi ashamed, you shall go upon the edge of the world and remain there until I send a messenger to you. You shall not know where on the edge of the world this messenger will come. You shall travel there watching for it until you have made a trail around on the edge of the world. When the messenger comes to you, you may then go upon the world and use your mysterious power to help those who are then to make the fourth time. When there is the fourth time, you will see your wife and your daughter with your grandchildren. Because of the power that Iktomi has given you, you shall live forever and shall be known as Wazi, the Old Man, the Wizard.

"Iktomi, as the offspring of Wakinyan who is honored most by words or deeds which are the opposite of the intent of those doing or saying them, you should have accepted laughter and derision as proper homage to you as a Sacred Being. You boast that by your power as a Spirit, you have brought shame to the chief of the Sacred Beings and the chief of mankind, and to the most beautiful of the Sacred Beings and the most beautiful of womankind, and that you will bring shame to all who have laughed at you. I give all power and I can take all power away or I can control it. Because you are the son of Inyan, you may keep your power as a Spirit, but you shall be no more associated with the Sacred Beings nor use your power against any of them. Mankind shall be warned of your tricks and all cautioned against you. You shall go upon the world and there abide alone forever without associate or friend."

Tate loved Ite and he wept and the people wept with him. He painted his face and the faces of his children black and stood before Skan and said, "Pity these, my children, for their mother was only a woman and could not know the consequences of her offense. Others caused her to forget the deference due to the Sacred Beings. Let her remain with her sons and let me bear her punishment."

Skan said to Tate, "My associate, because you still love this woman, you may go with your sons on the world and abide there where each of you may see Anog Ite as often as you wish, but you will be invisible to her until there is a fourth time. When that time is to be, I will send a messenger with a token. When you see this token, you will command your sons to establish four directions on the edge of the world, and when this is done, there will be the fourth time. You and your sons will govern the fourth time and then your sons will be messengers of the Spirits."

After that, there was the third time, a moon, and Hanwi governed it. She went from Wi, and never again remained with him. Ite brought forth her unborn child and it was a little son whose face she never looked upon, and Tate cared for him. She went upon the earth and made a tipi among the pines upon the shores of a lake. Wakanka went onto the earth and made her tipi beside a great spring which she could cause to flow hot or cold, as she wished. Wazi went to the edge of the world. He spoke often to the stars as they passed his path, asking them if they had a message for him. Iktomi went through the cave and onto the earth, where he talked with the birds and the beasts. He was always playing tricks on them, and all soon learned to avoid him, except the wolf and the coyote who often trapped him in his own mischief.

Tate gave a feast and invited all the Sacred Beings to it. When they had all feasted, Skan said, "The sons of Tate are born of a woman as no other Spirit has been. Therefore they are Kan, and they shall be like one Spirit. They shall be the messengers of the Sacred Beings, and in all ceremonies they shall have higher places than all the other Spirits, except my daughter, Woope. Tate's little son shall be a Spirit also. Because he is little, he shall be the Spirit of love and pleasure and all games. As Tate is my comrade, I will be the godfather of his sons, named Yata, Eya, Yanpa, and Okaga. But as Spirits they shall be named Tatuye-topa, the Four Directions. Tate's littlest son shall always remain with someone else so that he may have the care which a child should have, and his name shall be Yumnimni, or Yum. To them I give the powers to do the deeds they must do. They may go with their father and remain with him in the world until I send my messenger to him. Then they will begin their tasks."

The Fourth Time
and the
Four Directions

Tate and his five sons lived together on the world and their lodge was beyond the pines. Each day when Wi had finished half of his daily journey, he looked through the door toward the place of honor at the rear of the lodge. Tate sat at the place of honor, and Yata, his first-born son, sat beside him. Eya, the second-born son, sat at the side of the lodge on the right hand of Tate. Yanpa, his third-born son, sat at the side of the lodge on the left of his father. Okaga sat beside the door in front of his father. Yum sat at the woman's place beside the fire at the center of the lodge, but often he was with his older brother Okaga.

Tate did the woman's work around the lodge and his four sons grew strong and brave. But his little son, Yum, was always like a child. Yata was burly and morose. Eya was good-natured and careless. Yanpa was lazy and selfish. Okaga was kind and thoughtful. Yum was playful and thoughtless.

Each day when they had eaten, the three older brothers went from the lodge and wandered over the world. They returned only for their food in the evening and to sleep in the lodge during the nighttime. Okaga brought wood and water for his father and prepared the food for cooking. He played with little Yum and when he went from the lodge he took Yum with him for they loved each other.

Tate knew where the tipi of Anog Ite was. Unknown to her, he watched it to protect her from anything that might harm her.

One day when all his sons were away from the lodge, a shining star fell near his lodge, and Tate went to look at it. He found that it was a most beautiful young woman whose dress was soft and white. She carried a bundle which was decorated with many colors of mysterious design. He asked her where she came from and she replied that she came from the sky. He asked her who her people were and she said her people were the stars. He asked her where she was going, and she said that her father had sent her to the world to bring a token to his comrade. Then Tate knew that Skan had sent his daughter, Woope, as a messenger to him, and he knew that the bundle she carried was the token he was to receive.

Tate said, "I am your father's comrade and I will be your godfather. Live with me in the lodge as long as you wish, but do not tell my sons where you came from or who you are."

Woope said, "From now and forever more, you shall be to me like my father and I will live in your lodge as your daughter until I go away to live with another. Even then I shall be to you as a daughter." Then Tate led her by the hand through the door of his lodge and gave her a seat at the woman's place beside the fire at the center of the lodge.

He sat at his place and waited for the message she had brought to him. Meanwhile, he began to prepare a skin for a robe to clothe himself because he was naked. Woope asked him to let her do the woman's work and he gave the skin to her. She took from her bundle a sharp stone and quickly cut the skin into strange patterns. Then she took from the bundle a pointed awl and thread of sinew and quickly sewed the patterns together, making a robe. Tate wore this garment and he was comfortable and not ashamed.

He sat thinking until it was evening and Woope sat beside the fire place. Then came Yata. He thrust aside the door flap and saw his father and the woman. He went and sat outside and looked at the ground.

Next came Eya and flung up the door flap. He saw his father wearing a strange garment and he saw a woman dressed in white. He went and sat beside Yata and looked at the ground.

Then Yanpa came, lifted the door flap and put one foot inside the lodge. He saw the woman. He looked about the lodge and then drew back his foot and walked around the outside of the lodge. Again he looked inside and then went and sat beside Yata and Eya and looked at the ground.

Soon Okaga came with Yum and he said, "Ho! My brothers, why do you sit and look at the ground? Is there something that troubles you?"

Yata said, "It is our father."

Eya said, "It is the witch."

Yanpa said, "There is no food prepared."

Okaga said, "Is everything well with our father? Has the witch done him harm? I should have stayed with him."

Yum ran to the door and looked upon the woman. She smiled at him and he went inside, gazing into her eyes. Then he sat beside her and she put her arm around him, and he nestled against her, contented.

Okaga came and slowly drew aside the door flap. He looked first at his father and saw that he was smiling and happy. Then he looked at the woman and saw that she was young and beautiful. Her face was bright and shining and her hair soft, her dress white and clean, even her feet were clothed. He went inside and sat at his place and gazed upon the woman. But she did not look at him.

"She has bewitched our father," said Yata.

"She has placed a charm like a garment upon him," said Eya.

"She has made him forget to feed his sons," said Yanpa.

Tate heard them and said, "Ho! I should prepare the food!"

"I will do the woman's work, my father," said Woope.

Immediately a fire burned on the fire place and there were hot stones in it and water was in the cooking bag. Woope placed the hot stones in the cooking bag and said the food was cooked. Then Tate called his sons and said, "Ho! The food is ready. Come and eat."

"You are bewitched," said Yata.

"A charm is on you," said Eya.

"I am hungry and I shall go and eat," said Yanpa.

Yanpa went inside, sat at his place and looked at the woman. Woope smiled and Yum was contented, but Okaga was astonished by what the woman did. Tate called again and said, "My sons, come and eat."

"I will not eat with the witch," said Yata.

"She is not the Old Woman, so she cannot be the witch. Our father would not call us into danger," said Eya. Then Eya went inside, sat at his place and looked at the woman.

Again Tate called and said, "My son Yata, everyone is waiting for you to come so that we may all eat together."

"I will see her face to face and if she tries to bewitch me, I shall destroy her," said Yata.

He went inside the door and looked at his father and all was well with him. He looked at his brothers and all was well with them. Then he looked at the woman and she smiled at him. He crossed the lodge, sat at his place beside his father and looked at the woman.

"My father, what do you wish to eat?" said Woope to Tate.

"I wish for soup and cooked liver," said Tate.

Woope took from her bundle a new wooden bowl and platter. Then she filled the bowl with soup from the cooking bag and placed cooked liver on the platter. She gave these to Tate.

"My brother Yata, what do you wish to eat?" she said.

"I wish she would be our sister!" said Eya.

"I wish for soup and for flesh, both fat and lean, and for wild rice," said Yata.

Woope took from her bundle a new wooden bowl and platter. Then she filled the bowl with soup from the cooking bag and placed flesh, both fat and lean, and cooked wild rice on the platter. She gave these to Yata.

"My brother Eya, what do you wish to eat?" asked Woope.

"She is my sister!" said Yanpa.

"I wish for soup and a duck and cooked wild turnips," said Eya.

Woope took from her bundle a new wooden bowl and platter. She filled the bowl with soup from the cooking bag and placed a duck and cooked wild turnips on the platter. She gave these to Eya.

"My brother Yanpa, what do you wish to eat?" asked Woope.

"I wish for soup and liver and flesh, both fat and lean, and for a duck and for cooked wild rice and for cooked wild turnips and for pemmican," said Yanpa.

Woope took from her bundle a very large, new, wooden bowl and platter. She filled the bowl with soup from the cooking bag and placed upon the platter all that Yanpa wished for, and gave these to him.

She then took from her bundle a very small, new, wooden bowl. From her bundle she put into this bowl a little food, and told Yum to give these to Okaga. When Tate saw this he smiled, for he knew many things that his sons did not know.

"I smell flowers," said Yata.

"I smell ripe fruits," said Eya.

"I smell good things to eat," said Yanpa.

"I smell sweetgrass," said Yum.

Okaga said nothing and sat gazing at the small bowl and the little food that had been given to him. Woope took tidbits from the cooking bag and fed them to Yum and he was happy. All ate heartily of the food that was taken from the cooking bag and were satisfied. Okaga tasted of the little food that was in the small bowl and it was good. He then ate it heartily, and it was very satisfying. He ate heartily of this food but it became no smaller. When he had satisfied his hunger there was as much food in the little bowl as when he began to eat.

"If you are not the witch, I wish that you could live with us," said Yata.

"It would please me to have you for a sister forever," said Eya.

"I wish that you would always prepare my food," said Yanpa.

"I wish that I could always see your face," said Yum.

Tate heard and saw, and he smiled, for he was pleased.

"My four sons, it is not proper that you should sleep in this lodge while my daughter lives in it. Go and lie elsewhere until a place can be prepared for your beds."

They went from the lodge and saw a new tipi standing nearby. When they looked inside it they found four beds prepared with soft boughs of cedar and robes upon each. Because of his birth-right, as first-born son, Yata had first choice and he chose the bed at the place of honor opposite the door. Next, Eya chose the bed at the side of the tipi on the right hand of Yata. Then Yanpa chose the bed at the side of the tipi on the left hand of Yata.

Each slept on his chosen bed, but Okaga did not enter the tipi. He sat beside the waters and made music with his flute that was very pleasing. Woope sat in the lodge beside the fire place and Yum sat beside her. She heard the music by the waters and she listened to it.

"Why do you listen so?" asked Yum.

"I listen to the call of my beloved," said Woope.

"I love you very much. Teach me how to call you," said Yum.

She put her arms around him and drew him to her and said, "Yum, I too love you very much and shall always have you for my little brother. Your brother Okaga will teach you the music of love and you shall be the Spirit of love. But you will always be a child and do childish things, even as the Spirit of love."

"I would rather be a child and be with you than be strong and healthy as are Yata and Eya," said Yum.

Tate heard and he smiled for he knew that this was a part of the message from Skan.

At that time Hanwi governed the night and Okaga sat and gazed at her face for a long time. Then he cried aloud and said, "Oh, Hanwi! The Spirits declare that you are the most beautiful of all beings. But I say Woope is the most beautiful for she is like the stars." Then Hanwi smiled upon him, but Okaga was very miserable. When the nighttime was nearing its end he lay upon his bed near the door in the new tipi.

When it was morning Okaga came forth to fetch wood and water for his father. But he found there was already much wood beside the door of the lodge and water in the bag. Woope was up, but she would not look toward Okaga. When all were within the lodge, Woope served them food.

"I wish that you would always live with us," said Yata.

"I wish that I could always have the food you prepare," said Yanpa.

"I wish to have you always as my sister," said Eya.

"I wish that I could always look upon your face," said Yum.

Okaga said nothing and all looked toward him so he went from the lodge. Yum followed him and said, "My brother, I love you very much. Our sister is very beautiful, very good, and very lovely. Why do you not speak to her? She cannot do harm to anyone. I love her and I wish that you, too, would love her. Then you and she and I would be very happy together."

"You speak as a child of things you do not know about," said Okaga. "Your sister is very lovely. She is like the stars, far above me. I am not worthy of her notice and thus she has treated me. She is right, so go back to her and do not bother me."

Yum wept and said to Woope, "My brother Okaga has always been kind and glad to have me with him. Now he is unkind and spoke roughly to me. I love him and wish that you, too, would love him. Then you and he and I would be happy together."

"Your brother Okaga is not angry," said Woope. "He is only troubled and should be left alone. Weep not, for he will comfort you. And you and he and I shall be happy together."

Tate heard this and he smiled for he knew that Woope was a messenger from Skan.

That day, the three older brothers loitered about the lodge. Each of them tried to help Woope with her woman's work and often they spoke in a friendly way with her. Okaga went out and sat among the pines looking far away.

When it was evening, all were within the lodge and Woope served them. They all were gay and happy, except Okaga, who was miserable, and Yum was worried. When it was nighttime all slept as before. As Okaga was lying on his bed in the tipi he saw the flap of the door slowly move aside. Woope stood there and smiled at him. He leaped toward her and would have grasped her in his arms, but there was nothing there. He looked everywhere through the tipi and found nothing there. Okaga slept no more that night.

When it was morning and all had been served, Tate said, "My sons, go away from the lodge today, for I wish to be alone with my daughter."

The brothers went away. Yata sat on a hill and watched the lodge all that day. Eya went shouting and singing, he cared not where. Yanpa went and lay in the shade. Okaga and Yum went together far into the pines. Sometimes Okaga was gay and sometimes sad.

When the brothers had left, Tate said to Woope, "Did your father send a token to me?"

"He sent this bundle as a token to you," replied Woope. "Take it and keep it. When you wish for anything you will find it in this bundle. My father said you would know his token because of its powers."

"Did he send a message to me?" said Tate.

"His message is this. Now there is no direction in the world, and your four sons must each fix a direction and establish it so it will be forever known. When each one has fixed a direction, it shall be his dwelling place. The directions must be on the edge of the world and each an equal distance from the one next to it. They must divide the edge into four equal parts and one part shall belong to each of the four brothers. They must go around the world on its edge. From when they start on this journey to when they finish it will be the fourth time, a year. You shall govern the fourth time, the year, and shall give as much of each year's time to each of your sons as you want. Let your sons prepare for their work, for when they go from your lodge to do it, they will live with you no more. When they have established the four directions and made the fourth time, then they will be as Spirits, and do as my father ordered them to do. Your little son will always be childish and timid, but he shall be a Spirit of love, of pleasure, of games, and he shall live with his brother Okaga who loves him and will protect him."

"But you, my daughter, will you go from me too?" asked Tate.

"I shall always live on the world and will forever be like your daughter," said Woope.

Then Tate bowed his head and sat in sorrow. For his wife, Anog Ite, had left him, his sons would go from him, and he knew Woope would live in her tipi with Okaga.

"Mourn not, my godfather, for my father will always be with you, and no one can undo his words and all must obey them. He will comfort you, and you shall have pride in the works of your sons," said Woope.

Then Tate lifted his head and sang a song of defiance to Ibom, the Spirit of evil and sorrow.

When it was the next day, Tate told his sons the message of Skan, and ordered them to prepare for their work. He told them that for four days they should make their preparations, and then go upon their journey.

"How shall I make my preparation?" asked Yata.

"How shall I know where to go?" asked Eya.

"How hard will the journey be?" asked Yanpa.

"Shall I be with my brother Okaga no more?" asked Yum.

Okaga gazed at Woope and said nothing.

"Bring me flesh and bring me skins, and I will do the woman's work for your preparations," said Woope.

"Go and you will be shown where to go. Your journey will be long, but you will be able to go all the way," said Tate.

"Yum, you shall be with your brother Okaga always," said Woope.

"Then shall I be with you no more?" asked Yum.

"Your brother Okaga and you and I shall always be happy," said Woope.

Okaga stared at her and went and sat by the waters. With his flute he made music that was loud and hopeful. All heard the music, and all looked at Woope and saw that her face was shining like the stars. Tate smiled, for he knew that Skan had ordered all things well. Yata scowled, for he was jealous of Okaga. Eya strode about and laughed, for he cared for nothing and for no one. Yanpa sat upon his seat and moaned about his task, for he was lazy. Yum danced around and around, for he was childish.

On the first day of their preparation, the four sons went to get what they would need for their journey. Yata was angry and could find no game. Eya was careless and could find no game. Yanpa was lazy and could find no game. Okaga went afar and killed an antelope. He brought it back and laid it at the feet of Woope. She neither spoke to him nor looked at him. Then Yata smiled, and Yum was worried. She quickly took the skin from the antelope and made a robe of it. She prepared the lean flesh and mixed it with the blood and chokecherries. She put the mixture in the bag. Then she shaped the bag as a pack and took a pack strap and bound it about the bag so that it could be carried.

Yata watched her work and tried to seize her, but he was powerless to touch her. Then he asked angrily who she was, and she replied that when he had done what his father commanded, he would know. He said that when he returned he would take her for his woman, to serve only him. Woope said nothing.

On the second day of their preparation, the four sons went to get what they would need for their journey. Yata came back to the lodge and watched Woope do her woman's work and so he killed no game. Eya shouted and sang, and he killed no game. Yanpa walked lazily about and he killed no game. Okaga went afar and killed a deer and brought it back and laid it at the feet of Woope. She neither spoke to him nor looked at him. Everyone stared at her. She quickly took the skin from the deer and made a robe of it. Then she did the same with the flesh of the deer as she had done with the flesh of the antelope.

Eya watched her work, and marveled. He asked her who she was, and she replied that when he had done what his father commanded, he would know.

On the third day of their preparation, the four brothers went out as before, but the three older brothers killed no game. Okaga went farther than before and killed a moose. He brought it back and laid it at the feet of Woope. She did as she had done before, and Tate began to worry. She quickly made a robe of the moose skin and a pack of the flesh. Yanpa watched her and asked her who she was, and she replied that when he finished what his father commanded, he would know.

On the fourth day of their preparation, the four brothers went for the last time to get what they would need for their journey. Again, the three older brothers killed no game. Okaga went beyond the pines and sat beside a huge spring, for he was very miserable and could not hunt for game. He saw a very old woman with a stick hobbling along, and when she was near him, she fell as if in pain. He hurried to help her and led her to an old smoked and ragged tipi near the spring. She then peered at him and said, "My grandson, you seem to be in trouble. Tell me your trouble, and I will give you all the help I can."

"How can you, an old and feeble woman, help me?" asked Okaga.

"By my magical powers. I am the Old Woman, the witch. See that spring that runs cold: I now command it to run hot, and see, it boils," replied the Old Woman.

Okaga then told her of Woope, and she laughed loud and long, and he was angry. But she said, "You are blind and silly. Go to your father's lodge and take with you only that one thing which pleases you today. Give it to Woope, and she will treasure it."

Okaga went toward the lodge, but he had nothing to give because nothing had pleased him that day. He sat by the waters and gazed at the lodge. When it was evening, he smelled an odor that was pleasant. Again he smelled it and it pleased him. He found that it was the odor of sweetgrass, and he gathered a wisp of it and took it with him. He came to the lodge, and everyone, except Woope, stared at him because he brought no game. Bashfully he offered the wisp of sweetgrass to Woope, and she took the wisp and smiled at him and placed it in the bosom of her dress next to her heart.

That night he sat by the waters and made music with his flute, which was loud and very pleasing, and Woope and Yum sat with him. Woope held Yum in her arms and smiled. Tate listened and looked, and lay down contentedly on his bed.

When it was morning, Woope gave to Yata the robe of antelope skin and a bag of pemmican. To Eya she gave the robe of deerskin and a bag of pemmican. To Yanpa she gave the robe of moose skin and a bag of pemmican. She gave nothing to Okaga.

Tate implored Skan to aid his sons in their undertaking, Inyan to defend them from danger, Wakinyan to make their journey easy, and Maka to help them to fix the directions correctly. Then he said, "Yata is the first-born son, and his birthright is that his younger brothers should obey and give him first choice in all things. My sons, go to the edge of the world where you will find a path. Travel upon it, and fix the four directions on the edge of the world so that they will divide this path into equal parts. Beware of Iktomi who is on the world to do mischief. When you have fixed the four directions, return to my lodge."

The four went, and Tate and Yum and Woope watched their going. When they were gone, Woope said to Yum, "Little brother, run, and when you come to the four give these to Okaga."

She gave to Yum a little bag shaped like a heart, and a little circle made of fur. Yum ran, and when he came to his brothers, Okaga said, "Is everything well with those at our father's lodge?"

"All is well at the lodge, but Woope told me to run and give these to Okaga," said Yum.

Okaga took the little bag and circle, and placed them next to his heart. The four went on their journey, and Yum looked toward them as long as he could see them.

For many moons, Wazi had traveled, making a path around the world at its edge. Here the stars are very near at the beginning and end of their journey across the sky. When daytime was finished and before nighttime began, Anpetu would signal to the stars by coloring the sky many colors, and they would come forth leisurely and begin their journey. When nighttime was finished, Anpetu would again color the sky, and the stars would leisurely go to rest, and then the daytime would begin.

Wazi watched the signals given by Anpetu, and he traveled his path as did the stars. He waited for a message from Skan that a star was to bring. Whenever a star came near him, he asked it for a message, but each told him that it had none. He saw that some of the stars never came down to the edge of the world. One of them never moved while the others moved in a circle around it. He thought these might be the messengers of Skan and he made a lodge on his path, placing it under the star that never moved. Here he watched the signals of Anpetu and traveled no more.

He sat beside his lodge each nighttime and lay within it each daytime. He was sitting by his lodge when a star appeared and said: "This is the message of Skan to Wazi. Anpetu will color the sky at nighttime when the stars shine brightly. When this signal is given, go quickly and find your four grandsons. Deal justly with them, and help them in their tasks, but do not travel with them on your path. Obey, and when they have finished their tasks, you may go about the world as you wish. But you have made your lodge, and it must be your living place forever."

When it was morning, Wazi rubbed smoke on his feet, and bound an eagle plume to each of his ankles. He went about the earth and traveled all that day, more swiftly than birds can fly. With each stride, he stepped from one hilltop to another one far away. When it was evening, he sat to rest.

On that day, the four brothers left their father's lodge and traveled all the daytime, not knowing where they were going, for there were no directions. When it was evening, they sat to rest.

The three elder brothers spread out their robes, undid their packs and opened their bags of pemmican. Okaga brought water and wood and made a fire. His brothers began eating, and made fun of him because he had neither food nor a robe. He wondered why Woope had not provided for him. Then he took from next to his heart the little bag she had sent to him.

Immediately, everyone smelled an odor that was very pleasing. Okaga knew it was the odor of sweetgrass, for he remembered the wisp he had given to Woope. Then he remembered the small bowl with the morsel of food in it she had given to him the first evening when she served them in his father's lodge. He opened the bag and there was a morsel of food in it. He tasted it and it was good, so he ate heartily of it. When his hunger was satisfied, there was still the same morsel of food in the bag. His brothers laughed at him and said that he only pretended to eat. Okaga smiled and said nothing.

As Wazi sat, he saw the fire that Okaga had made, and he went toward it. The four brothers sat around the fire as they had sat in their father's lodge. Okaga sat opposite Yata and saw Wazi approaching. He said, "Yata, someone comes."

"No meddler must hinder us. We will learn who it is and then drive him away," said Yata.

"He will want some of our food," said Yanpa.

"Give him none of the pemmican," said Yata.

Wazi came and said, "Ho, my friends, may I sit with you?"

"Who are you? Where do you come from? Where are you going? What do you want?" questioned Yata.

"I am an old man and very lonely, for I am the only one of mankind on the world. I come from afar, and I don't know where I'm going. I wish to help where I can help. I would ask for just a little, and I would give much," answered Wazi.

"What would you ask?" said Yata.

"I am weary and ask to rest beside your fire. I am hungry and ask for food," said Wazi.

"You ask much of us, for we have not sufficient food for ourselves. What can you give for what you ask?" said Yata.

"I will help you in your work," said Wazi.

"You are a feeble old man, so how can you help us in our work?" said Yata. "We will give you none of our pemmican until you give us something. Lie by our fire this night, and when it is morning, give us help, or begone and hinder us no more."

"My brothers, do not treat this old man harshly. I will care for him as long as he is with us," said Okaga.

"Let it be so," said Yata.

"Old man, sit beside me. I have a little food, and while I have any you may eat of it," said Okaga.

When they sat together, Okaga gave the little bag to Wazi, and he smelled it and said, "This is food that the Spirits feast upon, and give only to those they love."

"Can it be that she is a Spirit? Can it be that she loved me from the time when she first gave me such food?" said Okaga.

"It is so," said Wazi. "She who gave this provided for you more than for anyone else. Cherish it as you would your happiness, for it is made of love. Take as much of it as you wish, and it will grow no less. As long as you prefer it to any other food, eat heartily. If not, it will be like ashes in your mouth." He ate heartily of the morsel in the bag, and it grew no smaller. He gave the bag to Okaga and said, "Okaga, you have fed an old man and he will give you much."

The three older brothers stared at Wazi, and Yata said, "Who are you that you speak my brother's name?"

"I am one who would help you, Yata," said Wazi.

"Are you Iktomi?" said Yata.

"I am not Iktomi," said Wazi.

When the three older brothers wrapped their robes about them to sleep, they were afraid. Okaga said, "Old man, I have no robe to give you."

"Did she give you anything besides the little bag?" asked Wazi.

"She gave me a little circle of fur," said Okaga.

"Show me that circle," said Wazi.

Okaga gave the circle of fur to Wazi, and he said, "This is the fur of no animal. It is that with which the Spirits clothe themselves. They give it only to those whom they favor. Care for it as you would for your own skin. If you choose any other covering rather than this one, then the Spirit who gave it will bow her face in shame, and this will remain only a little circle of fur."

Immediately, the circle became a large fur robe, and both Okaga and Wazi lay upon it and covered themselves with it. When it was morning, the robe became a little circle again. Thus it changed as needed until the four brothers returned to their father's lodge.

When it was morning, Yata said to Wazi that he must help them in their tasks or leave them. Wazi told them that if they did as he told them, he would give them a great deal of help. But Yata was afraid that the Old Man was Iktomi, and their father had warned them to beware of him. Yata said to the Old Man that if he would show that he could help them, they would do what he told them. Wazi asked what they wished him to do. It was very hot, so Yata said that if he would make a shade for them that would last all day, then they would do what he told them. Wazi lifted his hands toward the sky and murmured a strange speech, and immediately dark clouds were all over the sky. The four were astonished and agreed that he had the powers of a Spirit. Then the Old Man told them that his name was Wazi, and that Skan had sent him to help them in their task.

Wazi told them to made a smudge, and then to rub the smoke on their feet. They did so, and Wazi bound an eagle plume to each of their ankles. Then he told them to come with him to the top of a nearby hill, and they went there. He told them that their feet were magical and that they could step from hill to hill as far away as they wished.

He asked them where they wished to go first. Yata said they wished to go to the edge of the world, because each of them was to fix a direction there. As he was the first-born son, he would choose the first direction as his own. He would have this direction under the star that never moves, where the shadows are the longest at midday. Wazi said he knew the path around the edge of the world and could guide them to it at its nearest place. When they came there, they would be at the place under the star that never moves.

He showed them a hill far away and told Yata to step to it. But Yata was afraid and yelled at Wazi, calling him Iktomi. Yata said that Wazi wished to destroy them and that he would have Wazi driven from them. Eya said that he would step to the hill, and Wazi told him to do so. He stepped, and immediately he was on the hill far away. Wazi then bade Yata to step, but he was more afraid and trembled so much that he could not stand. Then Okaga encouraged Yata and persuaded him to step. At last he did so and was beside Eya. Then Wazi bid Yanpa step, and he did so and was beside his brothers on the hill far away. Last, Wazi said to Okaga, "My grandson, we will step together all this day. Fear nothing that you may have to do, for she who provided for your journey will keep all danger from you."

They stepped, and were beside the others. All that day the four brothers and Wazi stepped rapidly, traveling more swiftly than eagles can fly. When it was evening, they were beside a huge mountain. Wazi told them to wash the smoke from their feet and take the eagle plumes from their ankles, and he burned the plumes in a fire that Okaga kindled. He said that on their journey they could not travel as they had done that day. They must go on foot from then on until they had gone on the trail entirely around the edge of the world. When they had done so, they would again be at this mountain, but on the other side of it, and he would again help them to return to their father's tipi. He told them that on the next day they should climb the mountain and go over the top and down the other side of it. Then they would be at the trail around the world and there they should fix the first direction.

Yata said, "My direction must be where the shadows are longest at midday, and I am entitled to the first direction."

"When you have fixed the direction, then you will see your shadows," said Wazi. And while they looked at him, he vanished. When it was morning, clouds still covered all of the sky. The four heard horrible sounds coming from the top of the mountain, which they could not see because of the thick clouds.

Yata said, "Those sounds are made by Ibom and terrible beasts. If we go upon this mountain, they will destroy us. That was not Wazi who brought us here, but Iktomi. He brought us into this danger to make us ridiculous and perhaps to destroy us. We should not do as he told us. We ought to seek some other way to the path around the world."

"The mountain is very steep and very high, and I would rather not undertake the hard work of climbing it," said Yanpa.

"We must do the work our father has sent us to do, and how do we know from where we have come or where we are going? We can go up to the mountain until we find danger, and then we can run from it," said Eya.

"My brothers, I will go before you," said Okaga, "and we will climb the mountain. If there is danger, I will shout a warning. Then you can turn back."

The three agreed to this, and Okaga gave his flute into the keeping of Eya and said, "If I am destroyed and you come again to our father's lodge, give this to Woope. And be kind to little Yum."

Then all began climbing the mountain. Okaga was far ahead of the other three brothers. When he came to the top, he examined it cautiously and saw a great level space. Upon this space was a great cedar tree and beside it a huge lodge with upright walls and no door or covering. He waited, watched, and listened. He heard the dreadful noises that came from this lodge. Then he remembered that Wazi had told him that no harm could come to him, so he went onto the space to cross the top. He moved cautiously, watching for anything dangerous. When he was near the lodge, a booming voice bellowed and said, "Who is this that dares to come onto my mountain and near my lodge?"

"A son of Tate going to do his father's commands," replied Okaga.

"Pass on, Okaga, son of Tate," boomed the voice.

He passed on, but his brothers near the top of the mountain heard the voice, and they were afraid.

"That is the voice of Ibom, the cyclone," said Yata. "He is an enemy of our father, and therefore our enemy. He knows our names, for he called Okaga by his right name, and Okaga told him that we are the sons of Tate. He is planning to get us all near him so that he can destroy all of us, for he destroys everything he touches. I shall not go to the top of the mountain."

"I will go and look at the top, and if there is danger, I will come back," said Eya.

He came to the edge of the space and cautiously peeped over it. He saw the tree and the lodge and in the tree he saw a huge nest made of bones. He waited and watched, but heard no sounds. He then carefully went onto the space and came near the lodge. The voice boomed and said, "Who is this that dares to come onto my mountain and near my lodge?"

"A son of Tate who desires to know more of you and your strange lodge and this great tree with the odd nest in it," said Eya.

"Eya, son of Tate, stay and learn what you wish to know," boomed the voice. Eya stayed.

"That is surely the voice of Ibom. He is holding our brothers and expects us to come. I shall not go," said Yata.

"Let us both go and peep, and if you wish, we can return down the mountain," said Yanpa.

After being persuaded, Yata agreed to go to the edge of the space. When they came there and saw Eya walking about, they called to him. He said that nothing had harmed him or Okaga, and that Okaga had gone on. Then Yanpa went onto the space, and Yata followed far behind him going very timidly. When they were near the lodge, the voice boomed saying, "Who are those who dare to come onto my mountain and near my lodge?"

"They are my brothers who go to follow our father's instructions," said Eya.

"Tell your brothers, Yata and Yanpa, to pass on," boomed the voice.

The two brothers passed on, but Eya remained.

"Eya, son of Tate, what more do you wish to know?" boomed the voice.

"I wish that you would come forth from your lodge so that I may look upon you. And I wish to know more about this strange nest in the large cedar tree," said Eya.

"I will come from my lodge, and you may look upon me if you so wish," boomed the voice.

"I so wish," said Eya.

Then from within the walls of the lodge, a swallow flew up and out and landed near Eya. Eya looked at it in astonishment and said, "How is it that such a small bird can have such a huge voice?"

"This lodge is the lodge of Wakinyan, the winged one, and that great voice is his voice. I am his messenger and forerunner. Whoever looks at him becomes a *heyoka* and forever after must speak and act in an opposite manner. Do you still wish to look at him?" said the swallow.

"If that is all the harm he can do to me, I wish to look at him," said Eya.

"If he is offended by you, he will glance at you with his eye, and like an arrow of fire, it will destroy you. Do you still wish to look at him?" asked the swallow.

"I will not offend him," said Eya.

"If he is pleased with you, he will choose you for his companion, and you must live with him always. Do you still wish to look at him?" said the swallow.

"Yes," said Eya.

"His companion must help him in taking all filthy things

from the world. Do you still wish to look at him?" asked the swallow.

"I am strong," said Eya.

Immediately there arose from the lodge a shapeless thing like a rising dense smoke. It was without a head and had an enormous eye and a huge beak. In the beak were teeth like cutting stones. It had no body, but it had great wings, each having four joints. Instead of legs or feet it had mighty talons. Eya stared at it in amazement, and then laughed as if it were something very amusing. Then he stood on his head and walked on his hands. He shouted at Wakinyan and defied him and mocked him, saying, "You pitiful thing, your small voice frightens no one. Your weak eye can hurt nothing. Your beak and your teeth are good for nothing. Your wings are only tattered rags. Your talons are nothing but blades of grass. I would be ashamed to be your companion. I do not fear you and want none of your help."

Eya did and said just the opposite of what he wished, for he had become a *heyoka*.

Then Wakinyan assumed the shape of a giant man and said, "Eya, son of Tate, cease as a *heyoka*, for I am now the spirit Heyoka. You have pleased me as Wakinyan, since I delight in contradictions. Go now, and with your brothers do the work your father has told you to do. Then return to your father's lodge, but you shall live with him no more. Your tipi shall be upon my mountain, beside my lodge. Together you and I will purify the world from all filthy things. We will sweep and wash it, and water the ground. We will cause all things that grow from the ground to flourish and bear leaves, flowers, and fruits. We will give nourishment to all that breathes and cause their growth. We will fight the Unktehi, the monsters that defile the waters, the Mini Watu that cause things to stink, and Gnaski, the demon who delights in filth. This has been my task from the beginning. Now you will help me, and all that breathe will be grateful to us."

Eya gazed at the cedar tree and the strange nest in it, and Heyoka said, "I chose the cedar tree for my own and have never destroyed it with a glance from my eye. This cedar upon my mountain is the first of all cedar trees, and has lived from the beginning, and will live forever. All other cedars come from it. It is *kan*. The nest in it is my nest. It is made of dry bones that have become stone. The huge egg in it is my egg. From this egg my young continually come forth. I use them as drum sticks and the drumming is like my voice. They are *kan*. When I drum with them, they become myself, so that while there may be many of them, they are all only one, and that one is myself. Consider well all that I have told you. When you return to me, your tipi will be prepared for you. Go now, and lead your brothers, for Wazi has taken the birthright from Yata and given it to you.''

Eya crossed the level space on the top of the mountain, and the swallow went with him to its border where it said, "When each of you four brothers has fixed a direction, he must place a stone there, which will become a huge rock that cannot be moved. He must watch this rock until a bird alights on it. The first bird alighting on it will be the messenger of the one whose direction it is. This bird and its offspring will forever serve as messengers from the four directions.

"The directions which you will fix will be the only things in the world that are immovable. When going toward any of these directions, mountains, valleys, rivers, forests, or plains will sometimes be on one side, and sometimes on the other, but the direction will forever remain in one place.

"You will overtake your brothers before they have come down from the mountain, but say nothing to them of that which Heyoka has told, for Wazi will inform them of it in good time."

Eya went down the mountain, and before he was at the bottom, he overtook his brothers. Yata demanded why he had remained on the mountain so long, and scolded him for it, but Eya said nothing in reply.

When it was evening, the brothers came to the foot of the mountain. There they found the edge of the world and upon it a well-worn trail, and Wazi was standing on the trail. He told Eya to place a stone there, and he did so. Then the brothers camped for the night.

As they sat before the fire, Yata said to Wazi, "You brought us into danger, and then left us to face it alone. We overcame that danger and are here without your help. If again there is danger, you will again desert us. When it is morning, you shall leave us, for you are a dangerous guide."

"When it is morning, I will leave you," replied Wazi.

Everyone slept. When Anpetu first signaled to the stars that the nighttime was ended, they all woke up, and they saw that the stone which Eya had placed on the trail had grown to be a huge rock.

Then Wazi said to them, "That rock is fixed there forever, and it marks the first direction. It was placed by Eya, and is therefore his direction. From now on and forever, his shall be the first direction, and he shall have first place in all things. To him is given the birthright of the first-born son, and each of you other three brothers shall be subordinate to him as you have been to Yata."

Yata rose in anger and claimed the direction, saying that their father, Tate, had told them that the first direction was his because of his birthright. He said that his father was a Spirit whose word was not to be overruled by a mere man like Wazi. He screamed at Wazi and approached him to do harm to him.

Wazi pointed his finger toward Yata and said, "I am your grandfather. By the command of Skan, I came upon the world to help you and to deal justly with you. Yata, you are the first-born son, and if you were worthy, you should have the rights as such. But you are a coward, and like a coward you have abused your rights by oppressing those whom you should protect. You are stingy and give nothing to those in want. Worst of all, the one who would be your sister you sought to take by force. Your pride makes you foolish in times of stress, and you are therefore unfit to lead or command. I have the powers of a Spirit by the command of Skan, and I give the birthright to Eya. Skan alone can restore it to you," said Wazi.

While he spoke he still pointed toward Yata, who remained as if without power to move or speak. When Wazi lowered his hand, Yata sat and wept like a child.

Wazi said, "You four brothers, go and travel together on this trail. I cannot go with you. When you come to where the shadows are longest at midday, I will be there. Yata will then fix his direction and it will be the second direction. He will forever have the second place in the order of power."

While the brothers looked at him, he vanished.

After the four sons of Tate had gone from their father's lodge to follow his instructions, Woope did the woman's work in the lodge. Tate sat at his place in the lodge and was comfortable. When the lodge was as it should be Woope and Yum sat on a hill and looked toward the direction where the four brothers had gone.

Woope said, "Tell me about your brothers."

Yum told her, "Yata is the first-born son and all his brothers must obey him. He is strong and he sits beside our father. He loves no one, and he says and does very disagreeable things. He always chooses the best for himself, and I think he hates me.

"Eya is the second-born son, so he sits at the right of our father. He is very large and very careless, and only wishes to have pleasure for himself. He never notices me.

"Yanpa is the third-born son, and he sits at our father's left. He is neither as strong as Yata nor as large as Eya. He is very lazy, very greedy, and very cross. He scolds me and makes me feel miserable.

"Okaga is the fourth-born son, but I think he should have been born first. His seat is beside the door of the lodge. He is very beautiful and very kind to everyone, and he loves me. He plays with me and makes me happy.

"I have often gone with him on his daily trips. When I became weary, he carried me. He told me stories, and taught me about the animals and the birds and where to find the flowers and the fruits. When we found berries, he would choose the largest and the best. He had a right to do this because he was my older brother. Then he would slyly change his portion for mine and tell me that the younger must always obey the older brother, and that I must take what he did not want.

"Before you came, he always helped our father in the work at the lodge. He brought the wood and the water and made the stones hot for the cooking bag, and he brought more game and fruit and more turnips and rice than the other three.

"He is very brave. Once he and I were sitting among the pines when we heard the giant, Ibom, coming. He came like a round, black cloud with his feet on the ground and his head in the sky. He came dancing around and around and at every step he would smash down trees and kick them out of his way. Okaga told me to hide behind a huge stone and he stood and faced Ibom. They fought fiercely until Okaga thrust a large splinter from a tree into Ibom's leg. Then Ibom bellowed and fled as fast as he had come. Okaga was faint and he fell to the ground, and I thought he was killed. I blew my breath into his mouth and nostrils and after a long time, he breathed. Then he smiled at me and I was very happy. I would not let him carry me any more that day."

For many days, Woope and Yum sat together. Yum told her of his brothers, always speaking most in praise of Okaga. When he spoke like that, Woope would put her arms around him and draw him close, and say that she loved him very much. Many times he would say, "I wish that I could always be with Okaga, and with you too, oh Woope." She would also say that she wished the same thing.

Yum was contented and merry, for Woope amused him and interested him with stories and games. She taught him how to play all the games and told him that he would be the Spirit of games.

One evening, when it had been almost three moons since the four brothers had gone from Tate's lodge, an old woman came and placed her tipi beside the waters. Yum, on seeing it, told his father, and Tate smiled, for he knew that Skan ordered all things well. He told Yum to be kind to the old woman. When it was nighttime and Tate and Yum slept, Woope went into this tipi and said, "Wakanka, I want to speak with you about the four brothers."

Wakanka peered at Woope and laughed, and said, "All is well with Okaga."

"I know that all is well with him, but I wish to talk about him," said Woope.

"You have fed the hunger of Okaga. Can't you feed the hunger of your own heart?" asked Wakanka.

"The eating is best enjoyed when shared with another," said Woope.

"I have watched Okaga and I will have pleasure in the feast that you desire," said Wakanka.

"Already I enjoy the food," said Woope.

Then for many evenings they talked of the brothers, always speaking most of Okaga.

When it was three moons of time since the brothers had started on their journey, Woope said to Wakanka, "It is not given to me to know where the brothers are or when they will return to their father's lodge. As a seer, you may know these things. If so, I wish you would tell me of them."

"They are making the fourth time," said Wakanka, "and Skan has given no one a knowledge of what that time shall be. I will give you a picture of where they are on the trail around the world. When they have completed the circle, they will quickly return to their father's lodge."

She gave Woope a disk of rawhide with the hair removed. The disk was colored green, the top was white, and the bottom red. On the left side was a picture of a mountain, and on the right the colors of Anpetu. At the center was drawn a picture of a lodge.

"The disk represents the world," said Wakanka. "The lodge at the center is the lodge of Tate. The white at the top is where the direction of Yata will be. The mountain on the left is where the direction of Eya will be. The colors of Anpetu are where Yanpa will fix his direction, and the red at the bottom is where Okaga will fix his.

"When a direction is established, a red line will appear on the disk, from where the direction is fixed to the lodge in the center. These lines will divide the world into four equal parts. Count the moons from when one line appears until another is shown, and the days from when the Four have completed the circuit of the world."

Woope took the disk and showed it to Tate. There was a red line on it from the mountain on the left in to the lodge at the center.

"But the line is to the place where Eya sits in the lodge!" said Tate. Then he knew that his first-born son had been deprived of his birthright, and that Eya had been given the first place forever.

When it was evening, he and Woope were examining the disk when another red line appeared upon it. It came from the white space at the top of the disk to the lodge in the center. They knew then the second direction had been fixed that evening and that it was the direction of Yata.

That night, Woope made the third notch on her counting stick. She had made one notch for each moon of time since the brothers had left their father's lodge. The next time she talked to Wakanka, she showed her the disk and the counting stick and said, "Wakanka, look. Two directions are fixed, and there have been three moons of time. Two more directions are to be fixed and that will require three more moons of time. Then, how many days will they travel until they come to their father's lodge?"

"I am the only one of womankind in the world," said Wakanka. "Whatever gives you pleasure pleases me. I wish to say nothing that will in any manner take from your pleasure. Come to me as often as you wish, and together we will count the time. If we do not count correctly, we will console each other when we discover the mistake. When the Four have completed the circuit around the world, we will know it. Then you must quickly make ready for them. Two days they had traveled when they came to the edge of the world. They fixed the first direction there."

Woope thought carefully about these words of Wakanka's. The next time they talked together, she said, "In two days they came to the edge of the world and fixed the first direction. For nearly three moons, they traveled to reach the place for the second direction. They must now travel nearly three moons to reach the place for the third, and nearly three more moons to reach the place for the fourth. Then in two days they can travel to their father's lodge. Thus, in a little less than nine moons they may return to their father's lodge."

"The daytime is a circle; the nighttime is a circle; a moon is a circle; and the fourth time must be a circle. Look at the disk," said Wakanka.

Woope looked at the disk. At its edge, a fourth part of the circle was colored yellow, from the first to the second direction.

"Why is it yellow?" asked Woope.

"Yellow is the color of Inyan," said Wakanka, "the Spirit that Tate begged to protect his sons. This yellow shows that they have such protection. Inyan, the Spirit of construction, destruction, and of protection, has placed his color on the disk. In this way he assures Tate that his prayers are answered."

Woope showed the disk to Tate and told him what the Old Woman had said. Tate replied, "I knew Wakanka before she came upon the world. Then she was the wisest of womankind and a seer. She foretold many things. Some of these things were not as she expected them. By the schemes of Iktomi, she was made to do evil things. Because of this she was banished from her people, the Pte. She was condemned to live alone upon the world until she could give pleasure to her grandchildren, who are my sons. As Wakanka, she has the powers of the Spirits, but she can use them only to make my sons happy. This disk shows that soon she will be allowed to use her divine powers."

"All this I know from my father," said Woope. "But why is a mere woman permitted to know what is withheld from me? Is it to make your sons happy? My desire also is to make them happy."

For many nights she did not sit in the tipi of Wakanka. She sat with Yum, looking towards where they last saw the Four. Yum said, "My sister, why do you appear troubled? Are you also going to leave us? Your trouble is my trouble. Tell me about it."

"My little brother, you are to be the Spirit of love. I love you and I love another. Can a mere woman's love take him from me?" asked Woope.

"I am to be the Spirit of love and the Spirit of games. If I play and am very anxious to win, I forget the rules and lose. Maybe it is so with love. You know that I am childish, and maybe I have made the process of love and playing games much alike. If you are too anxious, you may forget the rules and lose," said Yum. Woope put her arms around Yum and kissed him.

That night she sat in the tipi of Wakanka, and Wakanka said, "This night you shall see your lover." All that night the fire burned brightly in Tate's lodge, and Woope lay as if asleep, but she slept not at all.

Eya had fixed the first direction and Wazi had disappeared from the sight of the Four, and it was early in the morning. Yata said, "Now that old meddler has gone, and I hope we shall not see him again. We will go on our journey, and where the shadows at midday are the longest, I will fix my direction. We will call it the first direction. Let us hurry on our way."

"We will not depart until we see a bird alight on this rock, and then I will tell you when to start on the journey," said Eya.

"How dare you challenge the command of your older brother!" said Yata. "I say we will go without delay."

"My brother, it is the will of the Great Spirit, Skan, that I shall have the birthright of the first-born son," replied Eya. "I did not wish it to be so, but all must obey his will. I would gladly give it back to you, if Skan will permit."

"This is why you stayed on the mountain. You planned to take my birthright from me. I will not have it so. You must obey my commands!" said Yata.

"Let us not quarrel," said Eya. "Let us call upon the Sacred Beings to decide this, and I will gladly submit to their will."

"There is nothing to decide," Yata answered. "I am the first-born son, and the birthright is mine. No one can make me the second-born son. I command you three to come without delay."

"My brothers, what do you say? Shall we ask the Sacred Beings for their will?" asked Eya.

"I do not care what you do," said Yanpa. "I am only afraid we will not have enough pemmican to last for all our journey."

Okaga said, "Wazi told us that by the command of Skan he has displaced Yata and given the birthright to you. Wazi is only a man, and we do not know for sure that Skan commanded him to do this. Let us ask the Spirits if this is Skan's will. If it is not, we will obey Yata. If the Spirits say that Wazi was right, then we will obey Eya."

"Is not our father a Spirit? Is he not the comrade of Skan? Did he not say that you should obey me? Did he not declare that I, as the first-born son, had the birthright?" asked Yata.

"Okaga, call for the Spirits that they may tell us what is their will," said Eya.

"I command you to obey me and come without delay," said Yata.

"What do you say, Yanpa?" asked Okaga.

"I can lie and rest while you are waiting. So call the Spirits," said Yanpa.

Yata rushed forward in a rage as if to punish his brothers, but immediately Wazi appeared before him, and he stepped back and sat down.

Okaga made a fire beside the rock. When it had burned to coals, he took from the pack of each of the brothers a little pemmican and mixed it with a little of his own food. He put everything on the burning coals. When this made smoke, he prayed to the Spirits to decide for them who should have the birthright of the oldest son.

They all bowed to the ground and covered their faces. Soon they heard a small voice commanding them to look. They saw a swallow sitting on the rock. It spoke, saying, "The Sacred Beings have heard you and have directed Wakinyan, the Winged One, to decide for you. I am his messenger and this is the message he sends you. Skan has told his will to Wazi and no one can undo it. Wazi has dealt justly with you. It is the will of the Spirits that you obey Eya."

Yata grasped a stone to throw at the swallow, but he became like ice and could not move. Wazi said, "Because you are mean and ill-tempered, you shall always be like ice. When you come, things that breathe shall fly from you and all that grows from the ground shall be as if dead." Then Wazi vanished. Yata moved, but everything near him was cold.

Eya said to the swallow, "You are the first bird to alight on this rock. Are you my messenger?"

"I am the messenger of Wakinyan and of his helper," said the swallow.

When that daytime was ended, Wi went down over the mountain to his rest under the world. Eya said, "I give this name to my direction, Wi-goes-over-down."

When it was nighttime, Okaga sat on the edge of the world and made music with his flute that was very pleasing, and the stars that came near him paused to listen to it. Many of them clustered about him.

One bright star lingered near and cried a warning to the others, saying, "That music speaks of our sister. Don't stay near it, lest you be overcome by it." The others did not heed her and each longed to have Okaga for her own. Skan saw that they would not heed the warning and wished to trouble his daughter. He gave the music the power to melt them so that they became like a cloud.

Then he said to them: "Because you were willing to make my daughter sad, you shall be stars no more. You shall forever remain like a cloud which shall reach across the sky. You shall travel as before, but shall forever wander around the edge of the world in search of Okaga. But never shall you hear his pleasant music again. You will be a pathway from the world to the spirit land, but no one shall know where to find you except him into whose keeping I shall give you." And thus it is. Never again could they be like stars, but they always remain like a cloud which reaches across the sky. Each night they travel together, always wandering around near the edge of the world, searching for Okaga and his music. When it is nighttime, the end of this cloud is near the edge of the world, and that is where the Four are at that time. And it may be expected that they will come from that direction the next day.

When it was morning, the four brothers went on their way, and for many days they traveled on the trail. When it was one moon of time since they had left the tipi of their father, Yata said, "We have traveled far and yet we are nowhere. This is because Eya does not know how to lead. Had I my birthright, we would now have fixed the four directions, and be at the lodge of our father. When I led you, we went more swiftly than eagles can fly and were not weary. Now Eya leads, and we go laboriously, step by step, and we come nowhere. I should again lead you so that our work may be quickly done."

"My brother," said Eya, "our father told us that it was the command of Skan that we should make the fourth time which must be the greatest of all the times. See, it is but one moon of time. If we were to return to the lodge of our father, our work would not be done. Your direction must be on the trail around the world where our shadows are longest at midday. So we are going toward the place of your direction. Wazi caused us to travel swiftly when he was with us. He told us that he could not be on the trail where you must fix your direction. The Spirits have confirmed his word and we should not doubt it. We will travel as we have traveled."

Thus they went on for eight days and it grew colder each day. So each night Okaga made a great fire and the brothers sat about it. On the eighth night, there came an old man with his face covered. Eya told him to sit by the fire and asked him where he came from and where he was going.

"I know that you are weary," said the old man, " but I cannot travel on this trail with you. I come at night to amuse you so that you may forget your weariness." He sat beside the fire, and Okaga gave him part of his morsel of food to eat. When he smelled and tasted it he said, "This is the food that the spirits feast upon, and they give it only to those they love."

The brothers remembered that Wazi had said this about the food of Okaga and that he could not go on the trail with them. So they agreed that this old man was Wazi.

When the old man had eaten, he asked each of the brothers to lend him a moccasin. He placed the moccasins side by side. He showed them one white and three black pebbles. He juggled the pebbles in his hand and then quickly slipped one under each moccasin.

Then he asked Eya to juggle the pebbles, and he guessed, and guessed wrong. Yata then juggled, and again the old man guessed wrong. Then Yanpa juggled, and the old man guessed right. Then he guessed wrong for Okaga. Thus, they played this game far into the night, and the brothers forgot their weariness. Before it was morning, the old man said that if they would stay at this camp he would come the next night and teach them more about the game. Then he left them.

The next day the brothers stayed in that camp and when it was night the old man came bringing four bundles of wands with four wands in each bundle. He gave these four to the four brothers. He also brought a large bundle with four times four wands in it, which he kept. He taught them how to gamble wand against wand. They played the game, gambling the wands. They played far into the night and the brothers won all the wands.

Again, the old man asked them to stay at that camp so that he might come and teach them more about the game. Before it was morning, he left them. The brothers stayed the next day and played with each other. When it was night they waited for the old man but he didn't come. The fourth day they waited and played. Yata juggled only the black pebbles and won the wands from his brothers.

When it was evening Okaga made a huge fire. He forgot about his flint and tinder and left them lying on the ground beside the fire. When it was nighttime the old man came and everyone played.

Only Yata and the old man juggled the pebbles. Yata won all the wands because he slyly juggled only black pebbles.

As they sat beside the fire, the old man spoke privately to Yata saying, "You are the first-born son and should lead the brothers."

"You have given my birthright to Eya and he leads," said Yata, thinking it was Wazi talking.

"What would you risk to regain your birthright?" asked the old man.

"Anything and everything," replied Yata.

"I will play you three times. You may juggle twice and I will juggle once. He who wins twice will win our bet. I will bet your birthright," said the old man.

"What must I bet?" asked Yata.

"You may bet that flint and tinder lying beside the fire," said the old man. Yata slyly took the flint and tinder which Okaga had forgotten. He and the old man went away to gamble.

He juggled and placed only black pebbles under the moccasins. The old man lifted a moccasin and lost. The old man then

juggled and as he placed the last pebble under the fourth moccasin, Yata saw it was white. He watched the face of the old man
closely and pretended to lift the third moccasin. Yata then approached the fourth moccasin, and the old man appeared anxious so Wazi quickly lifted the third moccasin. There was a black
pebble under it and the old man won this game.

Then he said, "You have won a game and I have won a game.
Now I have one chance and you have three chances to win the
next game. When people talk about Yata, they will tell how he
gambled with me. Having your birthright will give you power to
command your brother, Eya. Then you may have revenge for
what he has done to you."

Yata juggled and placed only black pebbles under the moccasins and said, "I would bet more on this game."

"I should like to help you get even for the wrong that has been
done to you. I will bet my power as a Spirit against the woman
whom you desire," said the old man.

"Agreed, and I would bet even more," said Yata.

"I will bet my services to you against your seat with the Spirits," said the old man.

"Agreed," said Yata.

"You watched my face to learn when your hand approached
the white pebble, and now I shall watch your face," said the old
man.

Yata looked away from the moccasins while the old man pretended to lift each one by slipping his fingers underneath.

"You give me no chance and I will take no chance. I will close
my eyes and turn once around and lift the first moccasin my hand
touches," said the old man.

He did this and Yata watched him closely. He lifted the first
moccasin and a white pebble was under it. Yata stared in astonishment, and then he lifted each of the other moccasins. There
was a white pebble under each of them. He said, "You have
cheated me. These pebbles are all white."

"You should know that I have cheated. You put no white pebble under a moccasin. I should have taught you that the rules of the game are that if a player cheats, he should be cheated. I have played according to the rules and you cannot complain," said the old man. Then Yata wept as a child weeps and the old man laughed in ridicule.

When morning came, it was cold. Okaga wished to make a fire, but he could not find his flint and tinder. Then the old man laughed loud and long. He uncovered his face and said, "Your father warned you to beware of Iktomi. I am Iktomi and have made you ridiculous. Forever it shall be told that while you were doing the work of the Spirits you neglected it to gamble on a game of chance. Eya, your leader, permitted this to happen and even took part in it. Yata cheated and stole from his brothers and gambled away both that which was not his and that which he most desired. Okaga, the prudent Okaga, forgot his duty and lost that which was for your comfort. Everyone will laugh at you. Where you go, there is neither flint nor tinder. Each day, while you suffer, because you do not have a fire, I shall laugh at you."

The four brothers hung their heads in shame and Iktomi mocked and taunted them until Okaga made music with his flute. The music was very sad and Iktomi fled from it because he hated music.

That day the brothers journeyed on the trail. When it was evening, they were discouraged and cold. Then Eya prayed to Wakinyan and said, "Oh Wakinyan, we are comfortable and wish no help from you. The glance of your eye is cold and weak as fire. We scorn you and if you offer help to us we will not receive it."

The other brothers stared at Eya as if he were crazy because they didn't know what was pleasing to Wakinyan. All bowed and a small voice said, "This is the will of the Sacred Beings: Four days passed as you negected your work. Now each day you must travel a day's journey and a fourth of a day's journey to correct the fourth time. Do this four times four days. You neglected your work to gamble on chance, therefore when you are Spirits you shall be so uncertain that no one can tell where you come from, where you go or how you go.

"Okaga, by his neglect, lost the means for making a fire, therefore when he leaves his father's lodge for the last time, he shall never again make a fire.

"Because Yata gambled away that which was not his own, and even his desires, he shall have no seat with the Spirits. The woman's work shall never be done in his tipi, and he shall always be cold.

"Eya permitted gambling, which caused delay. Therefore, when he is a Spirit, he shall never lead in anything and shall do nothing wisely. By his scheming, Iktomi has made the four brothers ridiculous and interfered with the will of the Sacred Beings. So he shall forever fear fire and the smoke of fire.

"This is the message of Wakinyan: A dry stick moved swiftly against dry wood will make a fire."

The voice ceased and the brothers saw that a swallow had spoken to them.

Eya knew that Wakinyan had answered him. They got a dry stick and dry wood. Eya drew the stick rapidly across the wood, but there was no fire. Yata drew the wood rapidly across the stick, but there was no fire. Yanpa rubbed the stick rapidly against the wood, but there was no fire. Okaga held the stick and the wood and thought. While he thought, he twirled the stick with his fingers and saw that it moved swiftly. He twirled it between his palms and it moved more swiftly. Thus, he twirled the stick against the wood, and there was stuff like tinder. He twirled more swiftly, and there was smoke. The third time he twirled, there was a spark of fire, but it did not kindle. The fourth time, he twirled the stick with all his power and there was a fire which kindled. Then the brothers were warmed. They made a great fire, and when it was morning, there was a heap of burning coals. Iktomi came to bother them, but when he saw the coals of fire, he yelled in terror and fled from there.

For sixteen days, the brothers traveled a whole day and a fourth of another day's journey. They were worn and weary. It was three moons since they had left their father's lodge, and that evening Wazi was with them on the trail. He told Yata to place a stone on the trail. But no stone could be found because everything was covered with ice. So Wazi told Yata to place a block of ice on the trail, and he did so.

The lodge of Wazi was there beside the trail. Its poles were icicles and its covering was snow. He invited the Four to rest inside it, but they hesitated, fearing it would be cold. Wazi showed them smoke and sparks coming from the lodge, and they went inside and were warmed. When it was nighttime, Okaga made music with his flute, and the music was like pleasant dreams. The other brothers nodded as they sat, and then they slept.

"Lie on your robe outside the lodge. Speak no word before it is morning," said Wazi to Okaga.

Okaga spread his fur robe outside the lodge and wrapped it about him. It lifted and carried him as the clouds carry water, and it moved as swiftly as a falling star. Then it came to the ground gently. Okaga uncovered himself and saw that he was beside his father's lodge. A fire burned brightly inside it, and he quietly lifted the flap from the door. He saw his father lying at his place, Yum sleeping beside him, and Woope where the fire shone brightly on her face. Her eyes were closed, and she lay as if asleep. While he gazed at her, she smiled and was very beautiful.

For a long time, he stood in the door and gazed at her, and her beauty grew. Then he sat and made music with his flute. The music was like a dream of a whispered song of love. Very low and very pleasing he made the music, for he wished to awaken no one. Tate stirred on his bed, and Yum murmured in his sleep, but Woope lay as still as the dead. Only her eyelids quivered.

It was near morning, and Okaga forgot the words of Wazi. He reached his hands toward her and said aloud, "Woope." Immediately, his robe was about him carrying him as before. Woope sprang to the door, and then went outside, but could see no one. When she came inside, Tate and Yum were awake.

"My daughter, why go outside before it is morning?" asked Tate.

"I wish to do what is pleasing to those I love. Why are you awake in the nighttime?" asked Woope.

"I dreamed that a huge bird brought Okaga, and he made music with his flute. The music was like the music in my heart when his mother was with me," said Tate.

"I also dreamed that Okaga came. You and he made music together, and the music was such that I wished to hear it forever. Did you dream of Okaga, too?" asked Yum.

"I did not dream," said Woope.

When it was morning, Okaga was beside the lodge of Wazi. He made a fire inside it, and they ate their morning meal.

Wazi said, "Did you sleep well, Yata?"

"I slept cold, but I am refreshed. I dreamed that there was a sound as if a great bird left here," said Yata.

"Eya, did you sleep well?" asked Wazi.

"I slept well and am refreshed. But I also dreamed of a great sound. It was as if a huge bird came to this place," said Eya.

"Did you sleep well, Yanpa?" asked Wazi.

"I slept well and am refreshed. I also dreamed that a great bird went from here and returned to this place." said Yanpa.

"Did you sleep well, Okaga?" asked Wazi.

"I did not sleep, and I did not dream," said Okaga.

Everyone left the lodge, and they saw that the ice block which Yata had placed on the trail had become a great bluff. As they looked, a magpie came and alighted on it.

"The will of the Spirits is that the magpie shall be your messenger, Yata," said Wazi. "It is an evil bird, an enemy of all other birds. It is a thief, stealing where it can, and killing the young and helpless. It is a bird of ill omen, and when seen as your messenger it will foretell of trouble."

The magpie heard this and chattered loudly as it flew to the lodge poles of Wazi's lodge. Then it dirtied the inside of the lodge. Wazi scolded it saying,"Because you have done this filthy thing in my lodge, your young shall dirty your nest so that you must build a new one for each brood. When your nests are seen, it shall be said, 'The magpie is a filthy bird.'"

"Ha, ha! But no one will know which nest to search to find my eggs or my young," laughed the magpie.

Then Wazi said to the Four, "Rest this day in my lodge. You shall be refreshed as if you had not labored. I wish to hear again the music that Okaga makes with his flute, for never again shall the sound of it be heard at this place."

Inside the lodge, Okaga made music with his flute, and it was as if the grass was green, the flowers bloomed, and birds sang in the trees. All sighed in contentment. Then the music was as if Hanwi were showing her face on the world and smiling. It told of love and the comforts of a well-kept tipi, and all sighed with longing. Then the music was of triumph and well-accomplished deeds, and all sat erect, except Wazi.

He bowed his head, and said to the Four, "I am your grandfather. Your grandmother and your mother are on the world. We three were banished from our people, the Pte, because of the evil that we did. We are not permitted to see each other, and your mother is not permitted to see you until you have made the fourth time and returned to your father's lodge. Then we will be judged for all times. Do not delay in your traveling. Do your work well, for you will also be judged, each according to what he deserves. Beware of Iktomi, of the Unktehi, the water monsters, of Ibom, the giant cyclone, and of Gnaski, the demon. They oppose the Sacred Beings and may try to hinder you. I am no longer allowed to go upon the trail around the edge of the world, but I will be at each place where directions are to be fixed. There I will help and advise you and deal justly with each of you. I have refreshed you; Inyan will protect you, and Wakinyan will help you."

When it was nighttime, the Four slept in the lodge of Wazi. In the morning they were as refreshed and as strong as when they went from their father's lodge. So they went on their way, and each day when it was midday their shadows were shorter.

The morning after Woope had finished making the third notch on her stick for counting the moons, she happily did the woman's work and then went to the tipi of the Old Woman. Wakanka chuckled and said, "Your dream has made music for you."

"I did not dream," said Woope.

"He has fed you with the food of the Spirits," said Wakanka.

"He gave to me only as I gave to him," said Woope.

She showed Wakanka the notches on her counting stick and the lines upon the disk. While they were talking of the Four and their journey and of the fourth time, they heard someone outside the tipi. Woope looked out and saw a very handsome young man sitting beside a tree near the door. She went and spoke to him and he told her that he was lost and had traveled far, and was weary and hungry. She brought him some food and he ate and praised it, and said that if she would permit him to stay nearby and give him food until he was strong, he would serve her and do whatever she asked. Woope knew that it was Iktomi, and that he would try to make her ridiculous; but she let him think that she did not recognize him, and promised to give him food.

The next day he ate and was refreshed. Then he asked what he should do to serve her. She told him to bring back some game.

He went out and caught a rabbit and took off its skin, and filled the skin with bugs and worms and placed it inside his robe. "I will give this to Woope," he said to himself, "and then I will laugh at her and insult her, saying that she has bugs and worms for her food."

But the bugs and worms ate through the rabbit skin and bit his body so that there was only a little skin left on his chest. He came back without game, and was scratching himself. Woope asked him why he had no game, and why he scratched himself. He answered that he had trapped four fat porcupines and put them in his robe to bring back, but their quills had pierced the robe and his body so that he did not know when they escaped. He said that he had pulled the quills from his flesh and that made him itch.

Then she told him to bring water. He went and filled the vessel with water and then spit in it and defiled it.

"I will give this to Woope," he said to himself, "and then I will laugh at her and insult her, saying that she has vomit for drink." But the filth made the vessel soft so that it broke and spilled the water on Iktomi's legs, and made the skin on his legs soft so that it cracked and bled. He came back limping and without water.

Woope asked him why he had no water and why he limped. He said that when he came to the waters an Unktehi was there, and it fought with him and clawed his legs so that he was lamed and could get no water.

Then Woope told him to bring wood. He went out and gathered soft and rotten wood and bound a bundle of it with a pack strap. But the wood was so soft that it broke from the strap. He then bound the wood to his back, and said to himself, "I will give this wood to Woope, and when it smokes and burns her eyes, I will laugh at her and insult her, saying that she smokes her tipi with rotten wood."

He came with the wood and Tate, Yum, the Old Woman, and Woope awaited him. He tried to take the wood from his back but he had bound it so closely that he could not loosen it. He tugged at the strap and the wood began to burn on his back. He shrieked in terror and danced about with pain. All laughed at him, and Yum mocked him, saying, "Aha, Iktomi! You torture others to make them ridiculous, and now we laugh at you. "

Iktomi fled, for then he knew that Woope was more powerful than he, and could turn his own schemes against him.

The four brothers traveled for one more moon of time and came to a great lake which they could not see across. The trail between it and the edge of the world was very narrow, and there was danger of falling from it into the water. They couldn't make a fire that night and were miserable.

The next day they traveled in the same way, and a great beast came toward them from the water. It had a body like the body of a huge otter, a head like that of a huge wolf, and a tail like that of a huge beaver; and it had horns which it could make long or short as it wished. As it came toward them it groaned and growled and gnashed its teeth, and slashed the waters with its tail, making big waves. They knew it was an Unktehi, one of the water monsters.

When it was near them, it said, "Ho, sons of Tate! I will drag you under the waters, and instead of serving the Spirits, you shall serve me."

It rushed toward them and they fled. It thrust its horns at them as swiftly as a spear is thrust, but they dodged the horns. It continued to pursue them and they were nearly exhausted and implored Inyan for protection. Immediately there were great boulders on the path, and they leapt behind them. When the monster thrust with his horns, they struck against the boulders and were battered. This so enraged the monster that it came up on the trail and chased them away from the boulders.

Then Eya cried out, "We are safe from danger and wish no help from you, Wakinyan! Delay your coming, for we despise you! We are far from the great waters, and the Unktehi do not trouble us."

Immediately a dense black cloud was low over the water, and the Unktehi turned towards it. It was Wakinyan coming to help the Four. Then Wakinyan and the Unktehi fought. The cloud swirled and the waters were thrown high. Wakinyan flashed his eye here and there and bellowed his thunders. The Unktehi groaned and growled and snarled and thrust its horns into the cloud. It slashed the waters with its tail so that the brothers were nearly drowned. Then it rushed far out into the waters and went to its home at the bottom of the lake.

The cloud disappeared, and Eya mocked and ridiculed Wakinyan because he praised and thanked him. But the war between Wakinyan and the Unktehi still continues.

For one moon of time, the brothers traveled beside this lake, and now they came to a sandy region where nothing green grew and there was no water. All day they journeyed, and when it was night they had nothing to drink. In the morning they were very thirsty.

As they went on this way that day they saw a lake. Eagerly they left the trail to go toward the water. All that day they went toward the lake, and all day it appeared not far away; but when it was evening they could no longer see it, and Iktomi stood nearby, mocking and laughing at them.

"Ho! You sons of Tate! With your horrid fires you drove me away and you laughed at me. Here you cannot make a fire, and I laugh at you. With only a picture I have led you from your path and made you neglect your work. All day you have labored, traveling thirsty, going far from your trail toward a picture that moved from you as fast as you moved toward it. Ha-ha-ha, I see you burning with thirst and farther from anything to drink than when you left your trail. You laughed at me; now think of going back to your trail with nothing to drink, and then laugh, if you can," said Iktomi.

In the meantime, Woope and Wakanka talked of the Four. When Woope had made the fourth notch on her counting stick, she was thirsty and nothing would satisfy that thirst. She said to Wakanka that she feared Iktomi might have tricked the brothers and that they were suffering from thirst. That night, she sat beside the waters and drank from a shell, and her thirst was satisfied.

When it was morning, she went to the tipi of Wakanka, and said, "Rub smoke on your feet and tie an eagle plume to your ankles, and go quickly to the brothers. Take this shell and give it to them."

Wakanka did as Woope had told her. She traveled all that day, flying more swiftly than the water birds can. When it was evening, she was in a sandy region where nothing grew from the ground and where there was no water. She heard the laugh of Iktomi, and then she heard the music of Okaga's flute, and Iktomi laughed no more. She had found the brothers. They sat with their heads bowed in shame and weariness. Okaga was making music with his flute which was very sad and mournful, and Iktomi had fled from it.

When they saw Wakanka, Eya said to her, "Where do you come from and where are you going? Would you also hinder us?"

"I am an old woman who is very hungry," said Wakanka.

"We would help you, but we have little food and nothing to drink," said Eya.

She sat down. Okaga gave her some of his food. When she smelled and tasted it she said, "This is the food which the Spirits feast upon, and they give it only to those they love. The Spirit who gave you this food will also send you drink."

She ate of the food, and then took a shell from her pouch and drank from it. Then she gave it to Eya and said, "When you are thirsty, drink from this shell."

Eya put the shell to his lips and drank water from it. The water was cool and sweet. Each of the brothers drank from it until they were no longer thirsty. Then the Old Woman said, "For many days you shall travel where there is little water, and the Mini Watu, the water imps, have defiled what water there is. Let Okaga care for that shell. He should care for it as he cares for the food he eats. The one who gave one gave the other."

"Who are you who speaks my brother's name correctly?" asked Eya.

"I am a lonely old woman trying to make amends for the evil I have done. A Spirit knew of your thirst and told me to bring that shell to you. When you have fixed the four directions and made the fourth time, and have returned to your father's lodge, you shall see your mother, your grandmother, and your grandfather; then all will be judged for all times," said the Old Woman, and vanished.

The Four were thirsty no more. They had come to a place where the grass was young and the trees were budding their leaves. On the evening before the last day of the sixth moon of time since they left their father's lodge, there was no sunset. The four brothers were confused. The next day began before the night was ended; there was no dawn, and they were astonished. Again, night began before day was ended, and they were confounded.

As they groped in the darkness, they heard wailing in the nearby forest, and going toward it they found someone bound to a tree. They unbound him and asked him what his name was, and where he came from, and why he was bound. He replied that his name was Anpetu, the forerunner of the morning and the evening. Iktomi had tempted him into the forest to drink of waters that he said would make his colors more brilliant to light the sky at dawn and sunset. When he drank from the vessel which Iktomi gave him, he became powerless, and then Iktomi mocked and taunted him, took all his colors from him, bound him to a tree, and left him to perish. He said that he was afraid to return to his work without his colors. So Eya invited him to remain with them until it should be known what was best to do.

Again it was daytime without a dawn, and Anpetu hung his head in shame. All that day the Four traveled on the trail and Anpetu traveled with them. When it was night, without an evening, he wept loudly in the darkness. A voice said, "Weep not for that which your folly has caused. You shall know the judgment of Skan and then go your way."

The Four knew that it was Wazi who spoke. He directed Yanpa to place a stone on the trail, and they knew that they were where Yanpa must fix his direction. In the darkness, Yanpa could find no stone, so Wazi told him to plant a wand on the trail, and he did so. All slept there that night, and when it was again daytime they saw that the wand had grown to be a huge oak tree. While they looked at it, an owl alighted on one of its branches.

"It is the will of the Spirits that the lazy bird, the owl, shall be your messenger, Yanpa," said Wazi. "Like you, it prefers to sleep during the daytime, and its cry is dismal and complaining. In visions it shall be the foreteller of discontent."

The owl heard this and stared and said, "Ho! Ho!"

Then Wazi said, "This is the judgment of Skan. Anpetu let Iktomi trick him with a promise to increase that which cannot be increased, so he lost the unfading colors of the Spirits. Therefore, he shall labor morning and evening to color the sky, but his colors shall fade quickly. As they vanish, it shall be said, 'Iktomi again takes the colors from Anpetu.' Thus the folly of Anpetu will be remembered. Go now your own way and when mornings or evenings are gray, remember that you cannot get something for nothing."

Anpetu left them, and Wazi said to the Four, "No more shall I be with you on this trail until you are again at the first direction. When you are at the place where you have no shadow at midday, Okaga must place there on the trail a pink shell. Dangerous beings may hide beside the trail to harm you. Gnaski the demon, and Ibom, the cyclone, may molest you or try to draw you from the trail. Beware of their tricks and wiles."

He vanished and the Four saw him no more while they were on the trail.

Woope had invented many games and played with Yum. One day, as he was walking beside the water, it appeared as if Woope came to him with her face covered. She whispered, saying, "Come with me. I have a new game which I will teach you."

"I am glad to have a new game, but why is your face covered?" asked Yum.

"That is a part of the game, and you must have your face covered, too," she said.

"Why do you whisper?" asked Yum.

"That is also a part of the game, which you will understand when I teach it to you," she said.

She covered the face of Yum so as to blindfold him. Then she said, "Now we will walk to where you and Okaga played together, and then I will show you my game."

She led Yum, and they walked until Yum said he was very tired. She told him they would go just a little farther where they would be among the pines. Then he could lie down and rest while she taught him the game. So they went, until Yum said he could walk no more. Then she told him to take the covering from his face and lie down to rest. He did so, saying, "When you speak your voice is changed. You talk harshly, the way Yata talks. Why do you speak so?"

"You will understand why I speak like this when I show you my game," she said. "The game is this: you will have four guesses to find out why I speak in this way. Then I will have four guesses to say how you feel in this game. Now guess who I am."

"Are you not Woope?" said Yum.

"Wrong. Now I will show you my body and then guess again," she said. She showed him her body and it had many little scars as if bitten by insects.

"Are you the Old Woman?" asked Yum.

"Wrong. I will show you my legs and then guess again," she said. She showed him her legs and they had long scars as if clawed by an animal.

"Are you the wizard?" asked Yum.

"Wrong. Now I will show you my back and then guess again," she said. She showed him her back and it was covered with broad scars as if it had been burned.

"You are Iktomi," said Yum.

"Right! Now it is my turn to guess. I guess that you remember when you laughed at me and insulted me when my back was burning. That is my first guess. I guess that you are afraid. That is my second guess. I guess that you will be very lonely and very tired and very hungry before you see your father's lodge again. That is my third guess. I guess that you will always be ashamed when you think of learning to play a game from one without knowing who is teaching you or what the game is like. That is my fourth guess.

"Hereafter, when one plays a game with a stranger it shall be said, 'Remember the game that Iktomi taught to Yum.' You laughed at me when I was suffering and now I laugh at you. You, the son of a Spirit, will be the Spirit of games and of love; you will have the place that I had! But you are the son of a woman, and you shall govern by chance and by favor. You were not born as mankind is born and not even as your brothers. In games and in love no one can foretell what the result will be. As a Spirit, you shall be like a babe. For amusement you will risk anything. So it will be with those who pray for your protecting powers. You can protect nothing—not even yourself. To learn my game you have given yourself into my hands and now I leave you. Find yourself or let others find you. Ha-ha! Ha-ha-ha!"

Then little Yum wept, for he was very much afraid. Iktomi left him, but stayed just out of sight where his laughter could be heard until far into the nighttime. Yum didn't sleep that night and when it was morning he wandered, not knowing where to go. All day he wandered and when it was evening, he slept beside a spring of water.

When it was evening and Yum was not at his father's lodge, Tate was worried and Woope was alarmed. She went to the tipi of Wakanka who said, "Wazi comes and he will know what should be done. Yum has not gone by his own will. Anog Ite or Iktomi has taken him. Neither will do harm to him. Wait till Wazi comes!"

Woope didn't sleep that night. Late in the night, a voice outside the lodge of Tate said, "In the den of the wolf, near where Woope and Yum often sat, there the young one weeps because he is hungry."

When it was morning, Woope went early to the den of the wolf and in it she heard a faint cry. She dug with her hands until they were torn and bleeding. In the den she found only a young wolf. Then Iktomi stood near and laughed.

Immediately, Wazi was there and said, "Because of her love, a Sacred Being has torn her flesh and spilled her blood, the greatest sign of sincerity. Iktomi has insulted him who is to be the Spirit of love, saying that love, like games of gambling, is governed by chance. She who has shown this sign of sincerity is his teacher and she will enable him to make true love constant so that danger or even death cannot change it. None shall laugh at this, and even Iktomi is now ashamed of his laughter."

Iktomi sneaked quietly away. Wazi said, "This imp of mischief tricked you to do this work as he tricked Yum away from his father's lodge. This evening Yum will sleep beside the spring and Wakanka will go and fetch him."

Then Woope said to Wakanka, "Go to the spring and wait there for Yum. He will sleep there tonight. When he sleeps, bring him to his father's lodge."

Wakanka did this. As she waited beside the spring, Iktomi came to enjoy Yum's distress.

A doe came to drink and he said to it, "Give me some of your milk, for Yum comes and he is hungry. We will show the milk to him and then laugh at his distress."

"My milk is for hungry little ones. I would neither distress anyone nor laugh at anyone in distress. I will not give you my milk," said the deer.

A bear came to drink and Iktomi said to it, "Yum comes and is hungry. Give me some of the flesh you have buried and we will show it to him and laugh at his distress."

"I bury flesh to provide food for the hungry and I laugh at no one who is in distress. I will not give you any of the flesh I have buried," said the bear.

A she-wolf came to drink and Iktomi said to it, "Little Yum comes and is very hungry. Give me some of the game you have killed, and we will show it to him and laugh at his distress."

"I hunt only to satisfy my hunger and the hunger of my little ones. The bear takes that which I do not use. I love my little ones and so I would not distress any little one except to take it as food for my own. I do not laugh at anyone in distress, and I will not give you anything to make sport of any little one," said the wolf.

A coyote came to drink and Iktomi said to it, "Yum comes and he is very hungry. Bring me a rabbit. We will roast it and show the roast to him, and then laugh at his distress."

"Agreed," said the coyote.

He brought a rabbit and they roasted it. The smell of the roasting meat was good, and the coyote wanted to eat it but Iktomi forbade him. So he sat down and sang a song. It was so harsh and unmusical that it pleased Iktomi. The coyote sang more loudly and more harshly, and Iktomi was so pleased that he slept.

Then the coyote slyly took the roasting rabbit and hastily ate all of it except one hind leg. He crunched the bones and this woke Iktomi who said, "Because you have done this, you shall forever be hungry, and your song shall be disagreeable to everyone. You shall always be ashamed and not able to look anyone in the face, but will sneak about like a thief."

But the coyote laughed at Iktomi, because he was full and Iktomi was hungry; and since then, he does not sing, but when he calls he laughs, and his laugh is not pleasant.

Wakanka heard and saw all that was said and done, and she pronounced a spell against the remaining rabbit leg and stayed hidden. Soon Yum came, and Iktomi said, "Ho! Little Spirit of love, little Spirit of games! Do you like the game I taught you? Do you love me? Are you hungry? See, I have plenty to eat."

Then he greedily ate the remaining leg of the rabbit. When he had swallowed the meat, he clasped his stomach with his hands and groaned, for he was in great pain. Then he rolled on the ground and howled and did such strange things that Yum thought he was doing them for amusement, and he laughed long and heartily and forgot his weariness and hunger. The more Iktomi twisted himself about in his agony, the more Yum laughed.

Then Wakanka came and said to Iktomi, "Because you tricked this innocent little one, I have placed this punishment upon you. From now and forever, you shall hate the flesh of the rabbit and you shall have no power to beguile the rabbit. Whenever you see one, you shall remember the pains of this evening, and shall run from it. I will relieve you of your pains if you will take Yum in your arms and carry him gently to his father's lodge. Otherwise you shall suffer for a long time."

Iktomi eagerly agreed to carry Yum, so Wakanka caused his pains to cease, and they went to the lodge of Tate. As they approached the door, a rabbit hopped by them. Iktomi dropped Yum, yelled in terror, and fled. The coyote and his mate were near, and they laughed so much that it was as if many coyotes were laughing.

A fire burned brightly inside the lodge where Tate and Woope sat. They heard strange sounds outside and hurried to the door. Woope rushed to take Yum in her arms, and cuddled him, warmed him, and fed him.

Tate looked at the face of Wakanka and said, "Woman, I thought I would never see you again; but because of the help you have given to my four older sons, and because you have returned Yum to me, it shall be as if you had done no wrong to them or to me."

Wakanka said, "Since I was banished to the world, I have used my powers only to do good to the young and to punish the evil. I have been condemned to live forever, and I shall go on using my powers this way while I am on the world. You are the companion of Skan, whose judgment none can deny; I pray you to show him that I am determined to pay for my wrongdoing with good deeds. Ask him to make the burdens of old age light for me, so that I may help the young who deserve it."

"Do right because it is right, and not to gain for yourself, and Skan will know of it," said Tate.

When Woope's counting stick showed that six moons of time had passed since the Four had left their father's lodge, she looked at the disk and a third line was on it. Then she knew that Yanpa had fixed his direction and that only Okaga's direction remained to be established. Again she counted the moons. There were three moons from where the first direction was fixed until the second direction; there were also three moons from the second direction to the third. She and Wakanka talked together and planned how to welcome the Four on their return, and she notched the days on her stick. Often when it was evening she sat beside the waters where Okaga sat when he made music with his flute.

After Yanpa had fixed his direction, the brothers journeyed on the trail for one moon of time and came to a place where big trees of many kinds grew close together. All sorts of fruit were on the trees.

A beast shaped like a man came to them carrying fuits, and gave some to them. They ate and were refreshed. The beast told them that there was an abundance of such fruit not far away, and if they would give him some of their food, he would give them as much fruit as they wished. The three older brothers agreed to this, but Okaga would not part with any of his food. The beast brought back many fruits and took from them some of their pemmican.

Yanpa ate a great number of the fruits, and the beast told him that there was another kind even more delicious than any he had brought, but that the one who ate it must pluck it himself from the tree. His brothers would not go with him to get it, so Yanpa persuaded them to wait while he went for it.

The beast guided him through the forest for a great distance, until they came to a tree having fruits shaped like huge grapes. Yanpa ate some and they tasted sweet, but as soon as he ate them he fell asleep. When he woke, he was very sick and his mouth felt as if he had eaten something bitter. He felt that he hated food of all kinds. He looked around for the beast, but couldn't see it anywhere.

Then Iktomi appeared before him, laughing at him and taunting him, saying, "Yanpa will always be remembered whenever one neglects his duty to satisfy his desires, and it will be said, 'Yanpa neglected the work of the Sacred Beings to please his belly.' You and your two brothers traded your food for my fruits, and because of this your own food will no longer satisfy your hunger. All three of you may eat of your pemmican, but you, Yanpa, shall hate it; and all three of you shall be hungry until you return to your father's lodge. Now go, return to your brothers! There are three directions fixed, and they are at none of them!"

Yanpa got up, but he was lost, and did not know where to go. He heard a voice saying, "U-hu-hu-ah." He came to an owl and said to it, "My messenger, go to my brothers and go slowly so that I can follow you."

The owl flew slowly from tree to tree and Yanpa followed. He was very weak and weary, and when it was night, he stumbled and made noise. Then the owl flew lower and showed him the way so that he traveled more easily. Far into the nighttime they traveled and at last came to where the other three brothers had made their camp.

Yanpa said to the owl, "When you were made my messenger, you were called a stupid bird. Skan has so ordered it. But when I become a Spirit, I shall impart to you many secret things. You shall be able to see better at night than during the daytime. You shall fly so noiselessly that you may come upon your prey and it can neither see nor hear you."

Yanpa kept his promise, and that is why the owl now flies noiselessly and mostly at night.

The Four continued to travel on the trail. One night they lay down to sleep, and it was on the sixteenth night of the ninth moon of time. Okaga was wakeful, and he sat beside a small lake and made music with his flute. A voice answered him, saying "Ho-hu-wia. Ho-hu-wia. Ho-hu-wia. Ho-hu-wia." ("A woman's bones.")

"Whose bones are these?" called Okaga.

A voice near him answered, "The bones of her whom you love."

"Is all well with Woope?" asked Okaga.

"She is in distress in your father's lodge. Only you can relieve her distress," whispered the voice.

"What should I do?" asked Okaga.

"Go to your father's lodge without delay," said the voice.

When it was morning, Okaga told his brothers that he was going immediately to their father's lodge. Eya tried to persuade him to change his mind, saying that they would soon be where Okaga should fix his direction, and if he failed to do the work appointed by the Spirits, he would arouse the anger of Skan. If he returned to his father's lodge with his work undone, he would give up his right to become a Spirit. But nothing could convince him.

All that day he traveled alone, going toward his father's lodge. When it was evening he was at a wide, deep river. He placed his food and the little circle of fur on his head and swam the river. He had eaten nothing that day, and when he had crossed the river, he wanted to eat, and looked into the little bag, but there was nothing in it. He wanted to lie down and rest awhile, but when he spread the circle of fur, it remained only a little circle. He thought these things proved that Woope was in distress, and could no longer help him.

He continued on his journey during the nighttime. The next day he gathered roots and ate them, but they did not satisfy his hunger. When it was evening, he was at the foot of a huge mountain. All night he climbed it, and in the morning found himself in a dense forest. He traveled through the day, eating only berries and leaves.

By evening he was at a great swamp, and lay down to rest that night but he slept only a little. In the morning he saw many Unktehi in the swamp, but he boldly waded into it making music with his flute. The Unktehi gathered around him and followed him, but while he made music they did not harm him. All that day he waded slowly, playing his flute. By evening, he had crossed the swamp, and he was exhausted and lay gasping for breath.

The next morning he came to a great sandy plain where there was no water. He traveled on it and was very thirsty, but when he took his shell to drink from it, there was no water in it. He tried to hurry, but when it was evening he fell upon the sandy plain and knew no more till Wazi aroused him.

Wazi carried him into a dense wood, made a fire, and gave him food and drink. Then he asked him why he had left the trail and not done his work.

"Woope is in distress and only I can relieve her," said Okaga.

"Woope is distressed only because you have neglected your work," said Wazi.

"A whippoorwill told me that she needs me, and this bird does not lie. Unless I have word directly from her, I shall go to her," said Okaga.

Far away, at Tate's lodge, Woope sat beside the waters as she often sat in the evening. Here she had found a beautiful shell that had all the colors with which Anpetu decorates the sky in the morning and the evening. She kept it and used it as a drinking cup. Each time she drank from it she was reminded of the shell she had sent Okaga. When her notched sticks showed that nine moons and four times four days had passed, she sat and drank again from the shell, but the water in it became black and bitter. She cleaned the shell, but each time she drank from it, the water was black and bitter. She pondered about this, and then went to the Old Woman's tipi and told her what had happened.

"Your shell saved the brothers and put them on the right trail. Again, a shell will help him whom you love," said Wakanka.

"When it is morning, prepare as before, and go quickly to the Four," said Woope. "Give this shell to Okaga, and tell him to place it where he will fix his direction."

The Old Woman smoked her feet, put on the eagle feathers, and all that day she flew so swiftly that when it was evening, she was on the trail at the edge of the world. Three of the brothers were there, but Okaga was not there. Eya told her that Okaga had gone from them the day before, saying that he would return to his father's lodge.

The next day Wakanka traveled swiftly, searching for Okaga, but she did not find him. Again on the third day she searched, and when it was evening she was in a dense forest. That night, she saw a fire, and went to it. There she found Okaga, and Wazi was with him.

She came to the fire and said, "Woope sent me to you, Okaga, and told me to give you this shell as a sign that all is well with her. You should place it where you will fix your direction."

She vanished, and Wazi said, "Iktomi has fooled you by speaking when the whippoorwill sang. But he dares not come near this fire to laugh and insult you. Hereafter and forever, whenever the whippoorwill sings, it shall be said, 'True love is calling to its mate, and Iktomi shall not laugh.' When you come to the trail again, you will be where you left it. Then for twelve days, you must travel alone, each day traveling a day's journey and a third of another day's journey. Then you will be with your brothers and there you must fix your direction. Now wrap your robe about you and lie down to rest and sleep."

The little circle became a great fur robe, and Okaga wrapped it around him and slept.

For twelve days he traveled alone, a day's journey and a third of a day's journey, as Wazi had directed. In the evening, after the twelfth day, he was again with his brothers, and he placed the beautiful shell on the trail. They all lay down to sleep, and when it was morning, they saw that the beautiful shell had grown into a tipi that resembled the colors with which Anpetu decorates the sky. When Wi began his journey across the sky, the tipi shimmered in the light of day. A meadowlark sat upon it and sang like the music of Okaga's flute.

"My messenger, I will answer you in your manner of speaking, and pray that your voice may always bring pleasure as it has this day," said Okaga. He made music with his flute and it was like the music of the voice of the meadowlark.

The four brothers traveled from the shining tipi that fixed the direction of Okaga and went upon the trail around at the edge of the world so that their journey should make a complete circle. Then Iktomi sought out Gnaski and told him that if the four brothers completed their task they would become as Spirits, and forever oppose Gnaski and be his enemies. This enraged Gnaski and he told Iktomi to guide him to where the brothers were so that he could destroy them while they were still mortals.

When the brothers had traveled for one moon, Gnaski appeared on the trail before them as a huge shaggy beast with sharp horns, pawing the ground and bellowing fiercely. Eya, Yata, and Yanpa fled from the path, but Okaga stood while Gnaski glared at him. Then Okaga made pleasing music with his flute, and Gnaski bellowed less and less fiercely as he listened to the music.

Finally he came near peaceably, and said that he would follow and serve Okaga if he would often make such music. Okaga agreed and called his brothers, and they went on their way and Gnaski followed them.

For many days they traveled together, and Okaga made music with his flute, and Gnaski carried the loads of the brothers. When they had traveled for three moon-times after leaving the fourth direction, they came to where the first direction was established beside the great mountain on the edge of the world. They knew that their work was done, for they had gone completely around the world at its edge. But they did not know what to do next, so they stopped there, and Gnaski stopped with them.

Then Wazi came to them, and instructed them to go over and down the mountain and he would meet them again on the other side. A swallow came to guide them along an easier trail, and they climbed the mountain, Gnaski following them and carrying their burdens. When they came to the level top of the mountain Wakinyan roared thunderously from his lodge, and the swallow left them. The brothers stood in awe and Gnaski trembled with fear, for he was the offspring of Unk, and Wakinyan had declared never-ending enmity against her and her children.

Wakinyan rose from his lodge a shapeless being, gnashing his beak, flashing his eye, and thundering with his voice. The brothers fell face down to the ground, and Gnaski fainted with fright. Then a gentle voice spoke to them, and looking up they saw the amiable Heyoka standing beside them. He hailed them all as offspring of a Sacred Being, and told Gnaski to rise with no fear, because he had helped in the work commanded by Skan. He promised that because of the good he had done by carrying the brothers' burdens when they were worn and weary, the anger of Wakinyan would no longer be directed against him. To Eya he said that as the son of Tate having the birthright he would be chosen first in all that related to the brothers, and would be Wakinyan's associate in cleansing the world of evil things. To Yata he said that because he had lost his birthright by his conduct he would forever be the associate of the Old Man, the wizard Wazi, his grandfather, and be controlled by him. To Yanpa he said that because of his laziness he would always be disagreeable and have little pleasure. To Okaga he said that he would have that which he desired.

Then Heyoka was gone, and no one saw his going. The four brothers and Gnaski climbed down the mountain, and it was evening. Okaga made a fire as taught him by his father, and Wazi appeared among them, and all sat beside the fire.

Iktomi was watching and he was angry and jealous. In the morning when their fire was out he came and pretended that he was sorry for all he had done to try to hinder the brothers in their task. But Wazi knew he was still trying to trick them.

He said to Iktomi, "Skan has given me the power to help my grandsons in the work he wished them to do. So now I command you to bear their burdens in Gnaski's place. Since you know you have done evil, you must now do penance."

Then he made a travois of poles and a web of vines, and fitted it on Iktomi and made it fast with a harness so that he could not free himself. He told the brothers to place their burdens on the web of vines between the poles, and to travel on in the direction he showed them and they would come to their father's lodge. He then commanded Iktomi to follow the brothers, harnessed to the poles and pulling their burdens, and he told Gnaski to follow Iktomi and see that he did his penance. Then he vanished and no one saw him go.

The brothers traveled as instructed for many days. Iktomi followed them and the harness galled him and he was weary, but he could not loosen it. When he stopped to rest Gnaski would gore him. Iktomi raved at Gnaski but Gnaski laughed at him.

They came to a plain where little grew and there was no water. Here a gopher asked Iktomi why they traveled and where they were going.

"We go to where there is plenty of food. You would do well to follow us," said Iktomi.

So the gopher told his family and his friends, the prairie dogs and rabbits and badgers, that Iktomi had invited them to go with him to a place where there was plenty of food. All these animals took their families and followed Iktomi. An antelope saw them passing and asked a prairie dog why they traveled and where they were going.

The prairie dog said, "Iktomi has invited us to go with him to a place where there is plenty of food. It would be well if you should go with us."

So the antelope told his friends, the deer and the elk and the moose and the bighorn sheep. They took their families and traveled after the prairie dogs. A wolf saw them as they passed, and he asked why they traveled and where they were going.

A deer said, "There is to be a great feast and Iktomi has invited all the animals to attend it for there will be plenty of food of all kinds. It would be well if you would go with us."

So the wolf told his friends the coyotes, the foxes and raccoons, the skunks, the wild cats, the lynxes and the mountain lions. And all who were told took their families and traveled after the deer. An otter saw them as they passed and asked the coyote why they traveled and where they were going.

The coyote said, "The Spirits have declared a truce for all animals and sent Iktomi to invite them to a great feast where there will be plenty of food. It would be well if you would go with us."

So the otter told his friends the beaver and the muskrat and the mink and the weasel. All of these took their families and followed the coyotes. A turtle saw them as they passed and asked the muskrat why they traveled and where they were going.

The muskrat said, "The Spirits have called all the animals and reptiles to attend a great feast beside a lake where there is plenty of water and of food, and have declared a truce so that we may all live happily together. It would be well if you were to go with us."

So the turtle told all his friends, the frogs, the toads, the lizards, and the snakes, and all who were told took their families and traveled after the muskrats. A bear saw them as they passed and asked the turtle why they traveled and where they were going.

The turtle said, "The Spirits have called all the animals and the reptiles to a great council and a great feast beside a beautiful lake. They have declared a truce so that none may harm another. There will be plenty of food and water and good things for all. It would be well if you would go with us."

The bear asked, "Did Iktomi tell you this?"

"No, but he told the muskrat and the muskrat told me," answered the turtle.

The bear asked the muskrat if Iktomi had told him these things and the muskrat said, "Iktomi told the wolf and the wolf told the coyote and the coyote told the otter and the otter told me. So it must be so or so many would not tell it."

The bear asked the wolf if Iktomi had told him these things and the wolf replied saying, "Iktomi told them to the antelope and the antelope told them to the elk and the elk told them to the moose and the moose told them to the deer and the deer told them to me. If it were not so, so many would not tell it."

The bear asked the antelope if Iktomi had told him these things and the antelope answered saying, "Iktomi told the gopher and the gopher told me. It must be so or the gopher would not say so."

The bear asked the gopher, "Why do you travel and where are you going?"

"Iktomi said he is going where there is plenty of grass and he invited us to go with him," said the gopher.

The bear asked Iktomi, "Why do you travel and where are you going?"

"I usually travel for my pleasure and go where I please," said Iktomi.

"Have you invited others to go with you?" asked the bear.

"I invite all to do as they please," said Iktomi.

"All the animals are following you and saying that you invited them to a great feast and council," said the bear.

"All the animals may do as they please," said Iktomi.

"Would it be well for me to follow these animals?" asked the bear.

"You may do as you please," said Iktomi.

"Would I offend the Spirits if I should not attend this feast?" asked the bear.

"If you please to risk offending the Spirits, then do so," said Iktomi.

Then the bear called the other bears and said, "All the animals are following Iktomi to a great feast and a great council given by the Spirits. Iktomi is trying to keep the bears from attending so that the bears shall thus offend the Spirits and incur the enmity of all the other animals. He is jealous, because the bears are the wisest of all animals. We will outwit him and then laugh at him. Let us travel ahead of Iktomi, and when we have come to the place of the feast, the Spirits will see that we are the most prompt to answer their call and will favor us."

So all the bears took their families and traveled going before the four brothers and Iktomi.

Then Gnaski said to Iktomi, "All the animals follow us thinking that they go to a great feast. Let us tell them the truth and each will accuse the others of deceiving them and they will quarrel and fight and tear each other."

"I have told them only the truth. Tell them what you please," said Iktomi.

So Gnaski went to the bears and said, "The Spirits have not called a council nor a feast."

"Return to him who sent you and say that the bears are too wise to be tricked into offending the Spirits," said the bears.

So Gnaski went among the other animals and told them that the Spirits had not called them to a council nor a feast. Then the wolf stood up and said, "All the animals know that the Spirits sent Iktomi as their messenger to invite us to a great council and feast. Now comes Gnaski trying to persuade us to go back and to risk incurring the anger of the Spirits. We all know this demon Gnaski and that his delight is to cause others misery. If we do as he says, he will laugh at our suffering and our shame."

"What should be done to one who would deceive us?" said the fox.

"He should be punished so that we may all laugh at him," said the rabbit.

"Ho! Ho! Ho!" cried all the animals.

Then the bighorn butted Gnaski and knocked him down. The elk tossed him; the moose trampled him; the coyote bit him; the badgers clawed him; the beaver spanked him with his tail; the rabbit gnawed his ears; the turtle snapped his toes; the weasel sucked blood from his neck; the frog hopped on his face; the skunk squirted his stench into his nose, and all the other animals clamored to get at him. Gnaski fled as best he could. He staggered to where Iktomi was and Iktomi said, "I see. You told them the truth."

"I did, but I will never do so again," said Gnaski.

"Always tell the truth, but never tell the whole truth," said Iktomi.

Then Eya came and said to Iktomi, "We, the sons of Tate, go to the lodge of our father. Why do the animals follow us?"

"They are pleased to follow the sons of Tate who return successful from the work the Sacred Beings willed they should do," replied Iktomi.

"They think they go to a great feast. I tried to turn them back but they abused me," said Gnaski.

"Because you would deprive them of their pleasure, you shall serve them at their feast," said Eya, and went away.

Then Iktomi said again to Gnaski, "I told you: always tell the truth but never tell the whole truth."

Woope served Tate and he was pleased. She amused Yum and he was happy. One evening as she notched her counting stick she said to Tate, "Father, it is now twelve moons since your sons went from your lodge."

She and Tate looked at the disk and she said, "See! There are four red stripes from the border to the center which divide the disk into four equal parts. The four directions are established. The blue line around at the edge is a complete circle so the brothers have traveled on the trail at its edge entirely around the world and are now where Eya established the first direction. Their work is done and soon they will be with you in your lodge."

"Are the invitation tokens ready? Is all prepared for the feast? Let all who come take part in our rejoicing. The work is for the good of the world and all that are upon it. The will of the Sacred Beings is done," said Tate.

The next morning when Anpetu first announced the coming of Wi, Woope and Tate were awake and gazed toward where Wi goes over down to his rest. As they stood, a swallow came and said to them, "The Spirits have willed that I should be the messenger of Eya. He told me to bring you this message: 'Our work is nearly done and soon we will be in our father's lodge.'"

Tate and Woope sang for joy and little Yum skipped and danced. Soon all were busy at the lodge of Tate in preparation for the coming of the four brothers. That day they often stood and gazed toward where they expected to see the brothers coming. In the evening, they spoke little, and the next day they again watched and made ready. But the brothers did not come, and before lying down to sleep, Tate said, "Surely they will be here tomorrow."

For many days they watched and waited. At last Woope took the magic disk to the lodge of Wakanka and said, "Grandmother, the disk shows that the four directions are established. But it does not show where the brothers are nor when they will come. Tell me whether all is well or not with the sons of Tate."

"The will of the Great Spirit, Taku Skanskan, he that gives motion to all things that move, must be done. He will declare the completion of the fourth time," said Wakanka.

"But when will the brothers be at their father's lodge?" asked Woope.

"When you see the bears coming, then adorn yourself as you would have the sons of Tate see you," said Wakanka.

"Why do the bears come?" asked Woope.

"All animals will rejoice when the fourth time is established," said Wakanka.

"Will not the birds also rejoice?" asked Woope.

"When the meadowlark calls, then the birds will come," said Wakanka.

Woope told Tate all that Wakanka said and Tate said, "Let all who come with my sons be made to rejoice. A feast must be prepared for all."

Then Woope stood and said, "Oh thou, the Great Spirit, my father, help me; for many come with the sons of Tate and a feast must be prepared for all."

Wazi dozed beside a fire in his lodge when a light appeared and a voice said to him, "Go to the lodge of Tate and with the powers I have given you, help my daughter Woope to prepare a feast for all who come to rejoice with Tate and his sons because they have done the work that the Sacred Beings willed they should do."

Wazi smoked his feet and went swiftly to the center of the world where the lodge of Tate was, and with his magic powers helped Woope to prepare a great feast.

The bears knew when they were near the center of the world and went before the brothers so that they might be honored guests at the feast. When the bears appeared, Tate, Woope, and little Yum were happy and Wakanka and Wazi sang a song of triumph. Before they saw the brothers, Yum ran ahead to meet Okaga. Okaga placed little Yum on his shoulders and made music with his flute that was loud and joyful. When Woope saw Okaga and heard his music, she went inside the lodge of Tate.

When the brothers entered the lodge, little Yum ran to Woope, crying "Sister, here is Okaga!"

Woope gazed at Okaga and he gazed at her. She held her hand toward him and he sprang to clasp it. Then she put her hands on his shoulders and said, "Okaga, my powers have gone from me. Now I have only one great desire. That is that you may never go from me."

Okaga put his arms around her and said to Tate, "Father, this is your daughter. Brothers, this is your sister."

Yum danced, and Eya was boisterous with joy. Yata scowled and said nothing. Yanpa said that now they would have plenty of good food.

Woope said to Tate, "My father created me mediator and endowed me with such love as the Sacred Beings have. As one of womankind I came with his message to you and as a woman I have learned that love which you also learned, which mankind holds so precious. You and I are wiser Spirits because we know love such as men and women feel, and that is a tie which binds me to you as your adopted daughter."

Tate stood in the door of his lodge and sang a song. He sang these words:

"I am old.
A daughter is given to me.
A daughter at my age.
I shall not be naked.
I shall not be hungry.
My sons, hear me.
Let all hear me that have ears.
Cherish this my daughter.
Cherish her as your sister."

Then Woope called Wakanka and Wazi and Gnaski and Iktomi, and told them all to come inside the lodge, and she served to all within the lodge such food as each most desired.

The four brothers sat on their seats in their father's lodge and Eya told his father all of their journey on the trail around at the edge of the world, and all that Wazi had said and done, and how the birthright had been given him. Tate sat with bowed head and listened. Then he said, "Let it be so." To Yata he said that he forgave his faults of the past, for they had brought about his punishment, and it would be so forever. Then Yata stood and scowled at Eya and at Okaga and fled from the lodge.

All the Spirits came to the feast, but Skan said that the animals were hungry and should have their feast first. So the animals made a great circle, and Iktomi and Gnaski served them their food. When the Spirits sat in their circle Skan commanded the four brothers and little Yum to sit with them, and all knew that Tate and his four sons and little Yum would cease to be of mankind and become of the nature of the Spirits. Wazi and Wakanka served the Spirits as they did before they were punished; and all ate and were happy.

While they were feasting, Anog Ite, the Two-Faced Woman, appeared and asked if she alone of all creatures was barred from feasting with her mother and father, her husband and her children. Skan said to her that if her children honored her as she was then, she could have the pleasures they could give her. The brothers went toward their mother, holding out their hands to welcome her, but when they were near, she turned her hideous face toward them and they fled from her. Then she cried out that the curse was still upon her and that her only pleasure would be to torment mothers bearing children, and afflict babies with pains and fears; and she went away.

When she had gone, Skan said that at a feast it was good to give presents, and that those who sat in the circle of the Spirits could ask for what they most desired. He would give to each what he asked for, except to Tate and his sons. To Tate he said that he would again become the invisible companion of the Great Spirit and would nevermore assume the likeness of mankind. To the four brothers, he said that because they had established the four directions and the fourth time, the fourth time would be called *waniyetu*, the year, and would be divided into four seasons of three moons each. One season he gave in charge of each of the four brothers: to Eya he gave the first season, the second to Yata, the third to Yanpa, and the fourth to Okaga. He commanded each to govern his own season, all under the control of their father Tate. He said to the Spirits that from thence and forever, the four brothers would be as one Spirit, and the name of that one would be Tatuyetopa. To the four, he said that although they were as one Spirit, they would remain as four persons, and each must live near where his direction was established. Henceforth, Eya would be known as the West Wind and dwell in the mountains, where the sun goes to rest. His color is yellow. Yata is the North Wind; he lives in the cold region of the pines, with his grandfather Wazi, and his color is white, the color of ice and snow. Yanpa is the East Wind and lives where the great waters are, where Wi begins his daily journey. His color is blue. Okaga is the South Wind, and his color is red. He and Woope have their tipi in the center of the world where the sun is highest, and little Yum lives with them.

Wakinyan said that he had chosen Eya to be his helper in cleansing the domain of Maka of filthy and harmful things, and Skan said, "That is well."

Woope asked her father, "What of little Yum?" and Skan said that he would remain a child, but he was to be the Spirit of games, of chance, and of love, and would be known as the Whirlwind. Woope asked for herself that she might be forever the companion of Okaga, and Skan said that as the daughter of the Great Spirit, she should have all the powers and also be granted her desire. To Wazi and Wakanka, he said that in doing good for others they would be comforted, and in doing evil they would suffer.

When Skan ceased speaking, all the Spirits said, "Good, let it be so," and all the animals and birds, each in its own language, cried that it was good. When the clamor stopped, Skan said that the Sacred Beings would feast together no more and never again sit in their circle; that their communication with the people would be by visions, or through chosen messengers.

And so it is. And so it is that there are four times moving in circles: the daytime, the nighttime, and the moon-time, that circle above over the world and below in the regions under the world; and the year-time, that moves in a circle around the world.

The Coming
of the
Ikce Oyate

Since the Sacred Beings no longer visited them, the Pte people grew careless. They neglected the white fruits so that these became small and scanty, and the people were often hungry. After Wazi and Wakanka were banished to the edge of the world, their new leader was Tatanka. He was a wise man and he was able to communicate with the Sacred Beings, but the people did not listen to him.

Wi knew of all this, and he appeared before Skan and said that since Ksa, who was the Spirit of wisdom, had become the trickster Iktomi he was no longer one of the Sacred Beings, and many of the Pte people were doing foolish things because there was no Spirit of wisdom to correct them. Skan said that if someone could be found who knew how to do all things wisely, he would give him the powers of the Spirit of wisdom.

The great bear lay nearby as if he were asleep, but he was listening to the talk of the Spirits. He was very wise and had learned the secrets of the Spirits by listening in this way. He went to see the Pte leader, Tatanka, and said to him that if he would help him, they would teach the Pte people how to perform a ceremony that would please Skan. Tatanka agreed to help the great bear and to do what the bear would tell him.

So they made a rattle and a drum and composed a song and music for it. Then the great bear chose a place near where the Spirits were feasting. He began to teach Tatanka how to sound the drum and the rattle and how to sing the song. The Spirits heard the music and it pleased them. They came and stood near to listen to it. Then the great bear began to tell Tatanka how to make a dance lodge and how to dance in a pleasing way. He stood up on his hind legs and danced before the Spirits, which pleased them so much they gave him the name of Hu Nunpa, which means Two Legs; and they clothed him with long hair and warm fur so that his offspring ever after have such clothing.

Then in the presence of the Spirits, Hu Nunpa told Tatanka how a chief chould lead his people in all things. Tatanka then taught the Pte people how to make a dance lodge, how to sound the drum, sing the songs, how to dance, and how to act so as to do the will of the Sacred Beings. Then the Pte people had a great dance. When the Spirits heard the singing and the music of the drum and rattles, they came and joined with the people in singing and dancing.

Wi appeared again before Skan, and said that the Powers had argued among themselves, each claiming that he or she was best fitted to be the Spirit of wisdom; but each had declared that next after Skan and himself or herself, the great bear was the wisest of beings. So Skan announced that the great bear should be made the Spirit of wisdom, and that it must be done with due and proper ceremony. He called a council of the Spirits to do this and all were present.

Skan then instructed Hu Nunpa that he should be the Spirit of wisdom, medicine, and sorcery, and the protector of all holy men, medicine men, and magicians.

Now ever since the animals had tried unsuccessfully to choose a chief, they no longer lived peacefully together. After the directions and the fourth time were established, and when cold Yata blew from the north, the animals were often hungry. Iktomi whispered to the wolves that flesh was good for food, and the wolves began to kill the small animals and eat them. They grew fat, and the coyotes watched to see what they did, and began to do as they did. Then the other animals with fangs and claws did likewise, and the eagles and the hawks and the owls joined them. So the other animals, the diggers and the builders and the hoofed people, fled from them, and the animals and birds that took flesh for food had to hunt for it. Sometimes they still went hungry in Yata's season, and so they do to this day.

The bears are wiser than the others, so they eat flesh when it is easy to get, but they also eat fruits and honey, so when Yata blows his cold breath they are very fat, and they find a comfortable place and sleep until Yanpa comes bringing thawing winds from the east.

Iktomi was gleeful when he saw that he had caused discord forever among the animals and the birds. But now that he was made an outcast on the world, and the only creatures who didn't avoid him were the wolves and the coyotes, he schemed how to make use of them to help him to cause trouble and sorrow to the Pte people. He told the wolves that there were strange creatures in the regions under the world, and that their flesh was better food than that of any of the animals on the world. He said that he would help the wolves to induce these creatures to come up on the world where the wolves could have them for food; and the wolves agreed.

At this time, the only people on the world were Wazi, Wakanka, and Anog Ite, the Double-Faced Woman, who feared Iktomi because he had caused her so much shame and misery. When he appeared in the guise of a young man before her tipi, she knew who he was and went inside and drew the flap over the door.

He sat with his head bowed and his robe drawn over it as if he were in great sorrow. Many times she looked out and saw him sitting there. In the evening she went out and gathered wood near him, but he did not speak. At last she went to him and asked him why he sat with his head bowed. He told her that he was sorry and ashamed because he had caused her to suffer. He now wished to do whatever would please her. She said that nothing would please her until she could be with her own people. He told her that if she would tell him how he could bring her people to her, he would do so.

"If the Pte people taste meat, and see clothes and tipis made of skins, they will covet such things and come where they can get them," said Anog Ite.

"Help me to do this, and I will trick you no more," said Iktomi. And he has kept his promise, for never since that time has he played a trick on Anog Ite.

He called the wolves and told them that now he would help them to bring the people on the earth for their food. First he told them to make a drive for game and to give Anog Ite as much meat as she wished. They drove the animals and gathered many moose, deer, and bear, and killed them near her tipi. She dried the flesh and gathered much meat and made many robes and soft tanned skins. She made clothes for a man and a woman, and decorated them with bright colors. Then she made a pack of the clothes and choice bits of the meat.

Iktomi gave the pack to a wolf and went with it to the entrance of the cave that opens down through the world to the underworld. He told the wolf, "Go and watch the people under the world. When you see a strong and brave young man, speak with him alone, and give him the pack and tell him that there are plenty more of such things on the world."

The wolf went through the cave and saw the camp of the Pte people far away. Before it got to the camp it met a strong young man, who asked who it was, whence it came, and what it wanted.

The wolf replied, "I am a friend of the People, and I come from the world to give them what they most desire. What is your name, and what do you desire?"

"My name is Tokahe," the young man answered, "and I desire to be a leader of my people."

"This pack that I give you will cause you to become a leader," said the wolf. "Take it and show it to the people; let them taste the food and see the clothing, and tell them that there are plenty of such things on the world. You must not tell them how you got these things, and you must say nothing about having talked to me."

Tokahe showed the meat to the people, and they ate it and said it was good. He and his woman wore the clothes and all the people envied them. He told them there were plenty of such things on the world, and they asked how they could get them, but he could not tell them. Then an old man suggested that three men go with Tokahe to see these things on the world, so that the people would know whether Tokahe spoke the truth.

Tokahe chose three strong and brave young men, and when the moon was round, they met the wolf. It led them through the cave, which had many windings; and when they were on the world, it led them to the lake where Anog Ite had her tipi. Iktomi and the Double-Face saw them coming; she had prepared a feast of meat and soup, and Iktomi invited them to sit down and eat. Anog Ite covered her hideous face with her robe and appeared to them as a beautiful woman, and she served them with choice bits of meat and plenty of good soup. Iktomi appeared as a handsome young man, and he told them that both he and the woman were very old, but because they ate meat they remained young. Iktomi had told the wolves to drive the game about, so the young men saw many moose, deer, and elk.

When the young men went back to their people under the world, they carried with them meat, robes, and soft tanned skins as presents from Iktomi. He went with them to the entrance of the cave, and told the wolf to guide them back to their people.

Tokahe and his friends showed their presents to the Pte. They told them they had been to the world and had seen plenty of game. They also told them that the people on the world ate meat and appeared as young men and beautiful women even when they were very old. Tatanka, the Holy Man of the Pte, warned the people that these things were done by a wizard, and they wrangled, for some wished to follow Tokahe and some believed Tatanka's warning.

Tokahe said he would lead those who wanted to go with him onto the world where they could get meat and skins for clothing and tipis. Tatanka warned the people that those who passed through the cave could never again find the entrance, and must remain on the world. He said that the winds blew on the world and were cold; that game must be hunted, and skins tanned and sewed to make clothes and tipis.

Six brave men chose to go with Tokahe. They took their women and children and went from the camp, and the wolf met them and guided them through the cave, and then disappeared. At night, they came to a strange place and the children cried for food and water, but there was nothing to eat or drink. Iktomi appeared and laughed at their misery, and Tokahe was shamed. Anog Ite appeared as if to comfort them, but they saw her hideous face and fled from her in terror.

In the region under the world, Tatanka the Holy Man sought a vision to ask the Sacred Beings about the wolf and about Tokahe and his followers. He saw in his vision that those who went up through the cave would be changed and become a different people, and that they would forget the language of the Spirits and how to serve them. His vision told him that he must follow them, and that he too would be changed and become a shaggy beast and be known as the Buffalo, and he would have in charge the welfare of the people on the world. So in the morning when Tokahe and those who followed him were hungry and thirsty and cold, and did not know where to go, a great shaggy beast appeared among them, and led them to where there were fruits to eat and water to drink and trees and caves in which to shelter.

But they were changed, and when they tried to talk they found they had forgotten the language which they spoke before coming through the cave, and they had to invent a new language, that no other creature could understand. Only Tatanka remembered the language of the Spirits, and he alone could talk to the other creatures on the world.

Those who came up through the cave with Tokahe were the Ikce Oyate, the Real People. They were the first people on the world, and the Lakotas are their descendants.

When the Ikce Oyate first came upon the world, it was the time of Eya, the West Wind, and though the people were naked, they were able to live in the shelter of trees and caves, eating the fruits Tatanka had shown them. But when Eya's season was over and Yata came with ice and snow, the people suffered from cold and hunger. Then Wazi and Wakanka came to them. Tatanka the Holy Man had vanished from their sight, for he had become a

Spirit; but there were great bands of his shaggy beasts on the world. Wazi showed the Ikce people how to make fire, and how to make the bow and arrow, and to hunt the deer and the shaggy beasts they called *tatanka,* the buffalo. Wakanka taught the women to heat stones and put them into a cooking bag to cook their food, and how to tan skins and make clothing and tipis.

Now there were more people on earth for Iktomi to trouble, and he called the demon Gnaski to help him. These two assumed the appearance of young men, and came among the people. The Ikce Oyate received them joyfully, for they remembered how the Sacred Beings had visited them when they lived under the world, and thought these also would be welcome guests. They made a great feast for them, and Anog Ite came, covering her ugly face and showing only the beautiful one. Tokahe warned the people to beware of the strangers, but they paid no attention to him. The three mixed freely with the people, amused them with tricks and stories, and kept persuading them to continue the feast. Anog Ite talked with the women, and taught them gossip and suspicion; then she went among the men, tempting them with her beauty so as to make their wives jealous.

Tokahe observed that the dogs were hostile to these guests, just as they would be toward any savage animals. He again warned the people but they only threatened their dogs.

After many days of feasting, the people told Iktomi that their supplies of food were nearly gone. He laughed and suggested that they play the games that little Yum had taught them. He said that the people would lose their cares and bring luck to themselves. They chose sides and played until the people were weary. Iktomi was on one side and Gnaski was on the other, and Anog Ite acted as umpire of the games.

Then Iktomi proposed that they play for a wager, the stake to be a grand feast. If Gnaski's side lost, the people were to place all their supplies of food in that feast. If Iktomi's side lost, then the guests and the people would feast no more and would all work together to gather more food. Iktomi assured them that he knew where food could be gotten in abundance, and would tell them where it was. The people agreed and said that the side that won three games out of five should be the winner.

They played and Gnaski won the first game. They played again and Iktomi won that game. The third time they played, and Gnaski won. Iktomi won the fourth game. As they began the fifth game, all the dogs howled, and Tokahe began a strange chant, and the howling and chanting increased until this game was over. Gnaski lost it and Iktomi was the winner.

The people brought all that was left of their supplies of food, and prepared them for a great feast. After it was over, they asked Iktomi to lead them to where food could be gotten in abundance. He told them that when the birds fly before Yata, the cold North Wind, they are going to where there is an abundance of food, and if they would follow the birds, they would find the place. But now the people had nothing to eat and they were anxious.

Tokahe sought a vision, and in the vision he was told to follow a little snowbird. When he told this to the people, they were puzzled, for Iktomi had told them to follow the birds, and Tokahe told them to follow a little snowbird. As they discussed this, a magpie appeared in front of them all and chattered and squawked. Iktomi advised the people to follow it.

It was nighttime, and the next morning the magpie sat nearby, but a snowbird sat on the poles of Tokahe's lodge. The people made ready their possessions and followed the magpie, all except Tokahe. He sat inside his lodge and when the people were gone, Iktomi, Gnaski, and Anog Ite came and taunted him. They threw stones at the snowbird, but it persisted in returning to the poles of Tokahe's lodge.

All that day the people followed the magpie, through dense forest and over rough ground. When it was late evening, they came back to where they had started that morning. They were exhausted and hungry. Anog Ite appeared among them and said if they would follow her, she would lead them to her home where there was an abundance of food. Three young men promised to follow her. Tokahe warned them, but they mocked him, saying that they would follow birds no longer.

The next morning, Tokahe prepared his possessions and followed the snowbird. All the people followed him, except for the three young men who followed Anog Ite. All that day they followed the snowbird, going easily over smooth ground. When it was evening they came to a cave, and went inside it for shelter. Inside it they found a spring of good water. At that time, the squirrels, chipmunks, woodpeckers, and other creatures stored their supplies of food for winter in this cave. The people found this store and there was an abundance of food for them and for their dogs.

While cold Yata brought bad weather, the Ikce Oyate dwelt in the cave. When it was springtime, and ice had gone from the waters, they came from the cave. But things that grow from the ground had not yet sprouted and game was hard to find. In the small streams the dogs saw fish, and captured and ate them. Then the people caught fish, and cooked and ate them and found them good. So the people lived beside the waters. When the seeds of things that grow from the waters ripened, the people gathered them and found them good for food. In this way, fish and wild rice became food for the people.

Gnaski saw the people taking food from the domain of his mother, Unk, and he told her of this. She had appointed the turtles to be her assistants, and sent them to keep the people from getting the food from her domain. At that time, the turtle was a huge creature with long legs and could run swiftly. It had a loud voice and a terrifying roar. The turtles came and forced the fish to deep waters, and the people saw this and tried to drive the turtles away, but they turned on the people, roaring and snapping. Sometimes the Ikce Oyate fled from them, but they continued to gather the wild rice from the waters. Unk sent the turtles to complain to Maka that her creatures were stealing their food from the domain of Unk. Maka replied that mankind were the creatures of the Great Spirit and rightfully could take their food wherever it was found. Ever since then, the descendants of the Ikce Oyate take their food wherever they find it.

Anog Ite was kind to the three young men who had followed her. She showed them only her beautiful face, and provided abundantly for their needs as they journeyed for many days. But she led them first in one direction and then in another, and the young men didn't know where they were going.

They came to a dense forest where strange trees with strange fruits were growing. Wolves came and followed Anog Ite like dogs. In this forest, beside a broad lake, they came to her home. It was a den in the hillside. Here the young men ate and slept pleasantly the first night.

The next morning, Anog Ite ordered them to fetch fuel and water, make the fire, cook the food, clean the den, and gather fruits; and each day she ordered them to do all the work that had to be done. After a little time had passed, they said to her that they had not followed her to be her servants. Then she uncovered her hideous face, and they fled in terror; but the wolves chased them and drove them back to her den, and she laughed at them and commanded them to do her will.

Frightened by her horrible features and her insults, the young men planned to escape from her. In the evenings, they gathered by the lake where the eyes of wolves always gleamed as they watched them. Secretly the three prepared a raft of logs, and one night, when the wolves grew careless in their watching, the young men pushed the raft into the lake and steered it toward the opposite shore.

Late that night, Anog Ite demanded that the wolves tell her where her three servants were. The wolves howled a fearful challenge, and searched, but couldn't find them. Then Anog Ite ran swiftly around the lake with the wolves following her. In the early morning, the young men came ashore on the opposite side of the lake, nearly exhausted by their labor with the raft; but as they sat down to rest, they saw Anog Ite and her wolves coming, and they fled in separate directions into the forest. Two of them fell and were devoured by the wolves, but one escaped. His name was Wata. He wandered through the forest and came to a barren plain, and on this desert he wandered until he could go no farther because of his hunger and thirst, and he lay down to dream of his people.

As though in a vision, a wrinkled old woman staggered near him and asked him to help her. With his remaining strength, he supported the old woman to a hidden grove that grew around a spring of refreshing water, and in this grove was the old woman's lodge. When they arrived there, with amazing strength she lifted Wata and laid him in the lodge, and brought him food. She was Wakanka, the witch.

He told her his story and she gave him a token, telling him that it would point in the direction he should go to find water and food and to get back to his people. He traveled for many days, guided by the token, and at last came to the camp of the Ikce Oyate.

They received him joyfully, as if he had been dead and now came back to life; and he told them of Anog Ite and his escape from her. He told them that she feared nothing, except a lizard and twigs fresh from the cottonwood tree. Then the people chose Wata to be their leader, under their Holy Man, Tokahe; and ever since then, pregnant women of the Lakota gather fresh twigs from the cottonwood tree, and make images of the lizard for their babies to wear, as charms against the pains inflicted on them by Anog Ite.

The Ikce Oyate lived and multiplied, but the Mini Watu were in the waters, and when the people swallowed them they were afflicted with pains and fevers, and many people died. Tokahe sought a vision, and in the vision Tatanka showed him roots and herbs and taught him songs and ceremonies to be done. The men did as Tokahe taught them. In this way, a line of Medicine Men among the Ikce people was begun, and they continued and still continue to teach others their wisdom.

Tokahe also taught as he had been shown by Tatanka that if

steam enters the body, it will strengthen the person's *nagi* so that it can cleanse the body of any evil that torments it. If this steam is confined in a dome-shaped lodge, it will enter the body and it will exercise its powers to help the *nagi* in maintaining health.

Tokahe instructed the Medicine Men how to make a lodge so that steam could not escape from it. They found that when steam was made by hot stones in such a lodge, their medicine was effective, if it was followed by the proper rites and ceremonies. They found that it helped the *nagi* because harmful things were washed from the body during the sweating. The inner parts as well as the outer parts of the body were cleansed. So they named such a lodge *inipiti*, which means life-giving lodge, or lodge of refreshment.

Ever since then, when the Lakota are afflicted by disease, weariness, or sadness, they can refresh themselves in the *inipiti* with the steam and proper ceremonies inside the lodge.

Once a young man mocked Tokahe, and when Tokahe admonished him, he laughed. When the young man sat down, Tokahe held his hand over him, and said that he would now be like the dogs. The young man laughed in scorn, but when he tried to stand up, he could not rise, and when he tried to walk, he went on his hands and knees. He could only lap water with his tongue when he wished to drink. When dogs came near him, he snarled and snapped at them.

The people saw this and they feared this man-dog, so he had no one as a friend. After a time, Tokahe came and the man-dog whined and howled and crawled to Tokahe's feet with his head bowed in shame. Then Tokahe painted a red stripe across his forehead and said, "You shall be my Hunka (adopted relative) and your name will be Sunk. You will be to me like my son and will follow me." And Sunk followed Tokahe.

Tokahe taught him the mysteries that had been given by the Sacred Beings, and all their teachings. Then Tokahe chose another young man, whose name was Pahin, and he taught him as he had taught Sunk.When these two had learned the sacred mysteries and teachings, Tokahe told them to go separately to some hidden place and remain there without food or drink, and pray to the Spirits. If the Spirits granted them a vision, they were to return and tell it to him.

When they returned, Sunk said that a voice said to him, "The stone point of an arrow, the hoof of a deer, the quill of a hawk, and the root of an herb."

Pahin said that a voice said to him, "A tooth of a beaver, a claw of a bear, a talon of an eagle, the root of an herb."

Tokahe told them to go and get the things the voices had named, and to bring them to him. Then he told each of them to bring him a soft tanned skin of a young deer. Then he prepared an altar, by digging a square space of ground, four spans long and four spans wide, and pounding and leveling the earth. On this altar he laid the deer skins, and told Sunk and Pahin to place their hands on the skins. Then he put his hands on their heads and prayed to Skan, the Great Spirit. He told Sunk and Pahin that the skins were now made sacred, and must be touched only by one who was entitled to have his or her hands painted red because of some deed that pleased the Spirits. Next he told Sunk and Pahin to cut themselves and let the blood flow on each of the things that had been named by the voices they had heard.

When this was done, he told them that because their blood was their life, these things were now their blood-kindred; and because they had been granted visions, the Spirits were willing to accept them as Holy Men, and would communicate with them and give them powers to do what other men could not. He wrapped the bloody things in the sacred skins, binding them with special knots and chanting as he did so. He gave to each of the two the bundle that contained his blood, telling them that these bundles now had the power of the Spirits and must be reverenced as the Spirits are reverenced, and never entrusted to anyone else.

He taught them the songs and the prayers with which to call the powers of their bundles, warning them never to call them for any small matter but only to do the will of the Sacred Beings, which would be communicated to them. He taught them other sacred songs and dances, and they danced before the people.

The people watched with awe, and when Tokahe proclaimed Sunk and Pahin as Holy Men, to be reverenced and obeyed, they shouted, "Let it be so." Then they made a great feast, and placed Tokahe in the seat of honor, with Sunk and Pahin on either side.

When all had feasted, Tokahe placed his hands on Sunk's head and asked him what he saw. He said that he saw a strange people who did mysterious things and whose offspring were shaggy animals with hoofs and horns. Tokahe said that these were the Pte, who dwelt in the regions under the world, whom Tatanka had caused to follow him up on the world so that their offspring would be the buffalo that would exist to be food, clothing, and shelter for mankind.

Then he placed his hands on the head of Pahin and asked him what he saw. Pahin said that he saw a strange people who spoke a different language and did things the Ikce Oyate did not do. Tokahe said that these were those whom Iktomi and Gnaski had led astray, and had taught strange customs, a new language, and other Spirits so that they forgot the Sacred Beings of their ancestors.

Tokahe commanded the Ikce Oyate to continue to live as relatives of one blood, and if necessary to fight for their families and for the rights which the Spirits had given them.

Parents brought their sons and begged Tokahe to give them whatever would make them the men he wished them to be. He answered that only the Spirits could do that, and advised each one to send his son to a secluded spot to seek a vision. If one were granted, he would interpret it so that it could guide the conduct of the one who had received it, and honor would be given or withheld according to his following of this guide. Many people sent their sons to seek a vision and to many, a vision was granted: to some, it came as an animal or a bird speaking, to some as a voice, and to some as a sound or an image. These messages were all in the language of the Spirits, and Tokahe interpreted them.

Since that time, any ambitious youth who is a descendant of the Ikce Oyate seeks a vision as taught by Tokahe, and the Holy Men interpret whatever vision may be granted.

Then the mothers prayed to Tokahe to give their young daughters that which would make them good and true women. Tokahe taught a ceremony for a girl who has just arrived at womanhood, and decreed that any woman for whom the ceremony was performed should wear a red stripe painted at the parting of the hair, which would give her precedence over all those who did not wear it. Since then, any ambitious girl who is a descendant of the Ikce Oyate has the Buffalo Ceremony performed for her, and those who wear the red stripe at the parting of the hair have precedence over the others in all things.

Tokahe remained with the Ikce Oyate for many generations teaching them their customs and rites, and teaching their Holy Men. He did not suffer from any disease or pain or any harmful thing, but he grew withered and weak. He told Wata, the chief of the Ikce Oyate, to bring two poles and place them side by side. During the night, a huge spider came and wove a web between the two poles. The people were puzzled because this web was so strong. When the people moved their dwelling place, Tokahe sat on this web and Sunk and Pahin lifted the poles on their shoulders, and traveled more easily bearing the poles with Tokahe sitting in the web than if they carried no burden at all.

Tokahe told the people that he came from far away and must return there; that he came in obedience to the command of the Spirits, and would go according to their will. Sitting on his magic web, he told Sunk and Pahin to carry him where he directed, and as he left, all the people bowed down with grief and chanted the songs for the dead.

Sunk and Pahin carried Tokahe to a place that no man knows. They left him alone, but they stayed nearby for one moon of time to protect him from harm. When they returned to where they had left him, he was not there, nor was his body there. Tokahe was seen no more by anyone. The teachings he gave are considered as binding upon the true descendants of the Ikce Oyate even to this day.

Epilogue
The Sacred Pipe

The Ikce Oyate lived and grew strong through good years and bad years, and Wakan Tanka, the Four that are One, continued to watch over them from above. Long, long after the days of To-kahe, Woope the beautiful was sent once more by her father to visit the people and to help them ...

It was a year of hunger and hardship for the Ikce people; the men had hunted in vain for buffalo, and the small game was scarce. One day two men were hunting together and as they came to a hilltop, they saw something approaching from the west which they could not see clearly. At first it seemed to be a solitary buffalo, and then it looked like a person. At last it drew near and they saw it was a beautiful woman, carrying something in her hands. As she approached them, one of the men knew she was a Holy Being and he stood still and waited. The other looked on her with lust, and started forward to take hold of her. At that moment a cloud enveloped him and the woman so they were hidden from his companion, and when the cloud dissolved, the woman stood alone and on the ground lay a skeleton.

Then the woman spoke to the other young man and told him to go back to his people and to tell them to prepare in a certain way a lodge and an altar of mellowed earth facing the west, and to wait for her coming.

The young man ran back to the camp, running zigzag as he approached it to let the people know that he was a scout returning with news. He told the chiefs and the old men what had happened. Quickly they prepared the lodge as the woman had told them, and at sunrise she came and walked into the camp and entered the lodge and sat in the place of honor. The chief greeted her as a sister and a messenger from the Sacred Beings, and offered her a braid of sweetgrass dipped in water to drink, and she received it.

The woman told them she was their sister and had been sent to help them. She told them to send out scouts and to prepare for a hunt. The scouts found a great herd of buffalo and drove it toward the camp, and the people killed all the animals that they needed.

Then the woman spoke to the people and showed them the pipe that she was carrying. She told them that it was a present from the Buffalo People, and that they were to use it to pray and to make peace. She spoke to the women as her sisters, and told them that they were chosen by Wakan Tanka to feel sorrow and love and care for the family, and to remember the dead. She spoke to the children and told them they were cared for, and must respect the Sacred Beings and the sacred pipe and be worthy of them. She spoke to the men as her brothers and told them how to use the pipe to protect and feed their people.

Putting tobacco in the pipe, she told them that the pipe bowl of red stone was like the body and was the container of all the good things of the earth. The smoke coming through the pipe stem was the breath offered in prayer. Lighting the tobacco, she offered the pipe to the sky, the home of Wakan Tanka, and to the earth, Maka, and to each of the four directions and the four winds.

She passed the pipe to the chief, and said: "Now I have done the work for which I was sent, and I will go away." She went out of the lodge, not allowing anyone to go with her. The people watched her as she went; when she was outside the lodge she disappeared, and in her place there was a white buffalo calf that ran away over the hilltop.

The people use the pipe to this day the way Woope, the White Buffalo Calf Woman, taught them, and in every celebration of the Sun Dance she is there as the leader of the dance and the keeper of the Sacred Pipe.

Cover art by Arthur Amiotte
Designed by Sylvia Steiner
Typeset in Baskerville
by Ampersand
Printed on acid-free paper